Financial Literacy for Young Adults Blueprint

Step-by-Step Guide to Improve Money Management Skills, Gain Credit Confidence & Learn Simple Budgeting Methods for a Secure Future

Noah Clark

Published by
Sprague Brook Publishing LLC
Paperback ISBN: 979-8-9947643-2-9
Printed in the United States of America

Legal Notice

Disclaimer

Contents

Introduction

You open your banking app, and your heart sinks. Rent is due in three days. Your checking account looks like a desert: dry, empty, and a little scary. Maybe you spent more than you thought last weekend, or your paycheck hit late. Now you're wondering if you can cover groceries, let alone split the next round of bills with your roommates. It's stressful, it's real, and you're far from alone.

If you're reading this, chances are you've felt that anxiety. Maybe you've wondered why money feels so complicated, or wished someone would just explain it without making you feel bad or lost. I get it. I've been there, too, not just as a young adult trying to figure out how to pay for life, but as someone who's watched friends and family go through the same maze. That's exactly why I wrote this book. I want to help young adults and the parents who care about them move from panic and confusion to confidence and results.

Let's be honest. Most of us never learned this stuff in school. The Roman Empire? Sure. How to build good credit? Not so much. No one pulled you aside to explain how interest piles up on a credit card or why your friend's "buy now, pay later" spree might come back to bite them. Instead, you were left to Google random advice, scroll TikTok for tips, or just hope for the best. But you deserve better.

Money stress doesn't stop at rent. There's the confusion about how to make a budget that works, one that doesn't leave you eating noodles and counting down to payday. There's the dread when you see your student-loan balance or the hesitation before checking your credit score. Maybe you've downloaded a budgeting app and felt completely lost within five minutes. And, all the while, social media is yelling at you to upgrade, travel, and post it all, like everyone else has life figured out except you.

Truthfully, almost everyone feels this way at some point. The difference is what happens next, and that's where this book comes in. I'm here to walk you through all that stuff that nobody explained, step by step. You'll find real stories, checklists, exercises, and scripts for awkward-but-necessary money talks. We'll cover how to build a budget that fits your life, how to use credit without fear, and how to understand student loans, and I promise you won't fall asleep halfway through the explanation.

This isn't another book full of recycled "skip the latte" advice. You'll get real, modern strategies that work for people with real bills and busy lives. You'll learn how to use the latest banking and budgeting tools, how to spot scams, and how to make fintech work for you instead of against you. By the end of each chapter, you'll have a clearer understanding of the topic and practical ways to apply what you've learned right away—no confusing jargon and no guilt trips—just real-world money skills you can use immediately.

Maybe you're skeptical. Maybe you've read other guides that felt too complicated or full of jargon. Or maybe you think you're just "bad with money." Let me tell you right now: You don't have to be a math whiz or make a ton of money to get this. You just need to start.

If you're a parent, you might be reading this because you want to give your child a better start than you had. You'll find plenty here to help you guide them through smart money decisions and start conversations that don't end with eye rolls.

Throughout this book, you'll get tools and strategies that fit real life, no matter where you're starting. We'll look at how to budget for surprise expenses, choose your first credit card wisely, and avoid debt traps that catch so many people off guard. We'll talk about recognizing financial FOMO before it wrecks your savings, and how to build habits that last. You'll also learn how to set up simple systems so you can spend less time worrying and more time living.

Money can feel mysterious, but it doesn't have to stay that way. By the end of this book, you'll feel more in control, less stressed, and more confident about your future. You'll have the tools you need, not a pile of generic tips that sound good but never actually help. You don't need to be perfect with money; you just need to be prepared.

And when you reach the end, take the quiz. You might surprise yourself.

So if you're ready to stop letting money control you and start making it work for you, let's get started. The next chapter of your financial story begins now.

Chapter 1

Rewriting Your Money Story

Mindset, Myths, and Motivation

E ver find yourself scrolling through transactions at 2:00 a.m., wondering why your bank account dropped so fast? Many people share that moment of panic, whether it's rent taking a bigger bite than expected, groceries costing more than your willpower, or that mortifying "card declined" message when you *swear* there was enough in there yesterday. These moments don't mean you're bad at adulting; they mean you're human. If money stress feels like a constant hum in your life, you're not broken or behind. This chapter will help you turn that anxiety into confidence, because money management is a skill you can learn.

Adulting Without Fear: Why Money Isn't Magic or Mystery

Financial literacy can seem like some mysterious power reserved for "finance people," but it's really just another life skill like cooking, driving, or setting up your Wi-Fi without calling your parents. You wouldn't expect to get everything right the first time, and the same applies to money. "Adulting" sounds intimidating, but it's mostly about taking small, repeatable steps, not leaping straight into millionaire status.

Think of budgeting like using Google Maps in a new city. At first, you're not sure where you're going. The app gives you a destination, a few routes, and off you go. If you take a wrong turn, you don't throw your phone out the window; instead, you stay calm and recalculate. Money works the same way. You start where you are, no matter how messy, and keep adjusting until you're headed in the right direction.

Everyone fumbles early on. One person might feel rich after their first paycheck until rent hits. Another might ignore auto-pay charges and quickly learn that overdraft fees are the bank's version of a "gotcha!" These setbacks sting, but people who start small, like tracking one expense or saving five dollars, quickly realize progress beats perfection.

It's easy to think "money stuff" is for older people in blazers, but look around: Plenty of your peers already use Venmo to split pizza, pay rent through apps, or invest on Robinhood. No finance degree required. They just tapped "download" and started experimenting.

Technology has made money management more accessible than ever. Apps like Rocket Money and YNAB (You Need a Budget) help you track, plan, and save, while tools like Apple Pay make checkout a one-tap event. You can literally build a budget while waiting for your coffee. These tools are made for everyone, not just spreadsheet lovers.

Many people avoid their finances because they're overwhelmed. But ignoring your bank account usually leads to expensive surprises, the kind that come with overdraft alerts and a small dose of shame. The good news is that tiny actions like checking your balance or setting up a low-balance alert can instantly boost your sense of control. Confidence doesn't come from being perfect; it comes from showing up.

Quick Check-In: Where Are Your Money Skills Already?

Give yourself more credit. You probably have more money skills than you think. For example, have you:

- Ever sent money on Venmo?
- Used an app to split bills?
- Compared prices before clicking "buy"?
- Gotten paid by direct deposit?

If you said yes to any of these, congratulations! You're already doing real-world money management. You're not starting from zero; you're starting from experience.

What matters most is starting now, even if it feels awkward or small. Each time you check your balance, log an expense, or resist pretending your bank app "doesn't exist right now," you're building momentum. The only thing that keeps you stuck is waiting for the perfect moment. But guess what? It doesn't exist. You don't need permission to start; you just need Wi-Fi and curiosity.

Busting the Top-Eight Money Myths Keeping You Stuck

Money myths are like bad hand-me-downs that have been passed around for years, slightly stretched out and totally outdated. They sound believable because you've heard them so often. The problem is, they hold you back before you even start. Let's tackle a few of those myths here:

Myth 1: "I'm just bad with money, so why try?"

After a bounced payment or forgotten subscription, it's easy to think you're hopeless. But nobody is born knowing how to manage money. It's learned, like riding a bike or folding a fitted sheet. Mistakes are part of the process. Try swapping "I'm bad with money" for "I'm learning new skills." Huge difference.

Myth 2: "You have to be rich to start investing."

A lot of people picture investing as suits and stock tickers. In reality, you can start with spare change. Apps let you invest with as little as five dollars. Waiting until you're "rich" is like waiting until you're in shape to go to the gym. That's backward logic.

Myth 3: "Credit cards are always dangerous."

Sure, they can be, but so can kitchen knives and trampolines. Avoiding credit altogether leaves you without a credit history, which makes adult life harder. Learn to use credit smartly, and it becomes a tool, not a trap.

Myth 4: "Budgeting means never having fun."

Not true at all. Real budgeting isn't punishment; it's permission. You can have fun; you just plan for it. Skipping the eight-dollar latte isn't mandatory unless that latte is drinking your retirement fund.

Myth 5: "Student loans will ruin my future."

Student debt is stressful, but it isn't forever. Plenty of people with loans buy homes, travel, and live great lives. The real issue isn't the loan; it's ignoring it. Missed payments do more harm than facing them head-on.

Myth 6: "Everyone should save 30% of their income."

That sounds nice in theory, but it doesn't work for everyone. If you're just starting out, saving even 10 dollars a week counts. The habit matters more than the percentage.

Myth 7: "My parents never taught me, so I'll never get it."

Lots of parents skipped Money 101 themselves. Financial literacy isn't genetic; it's learned. You're proof that learning can start anytime.

Myth 8: "All financial advice is outdated or for boomers."

Not everything from the 1980s applies today, but ignoring all advice means missing out on tools made for you. Apps, alerts, and automation exist for a reason. Use them.

Everyone makes money mistakes: overdrafts, late fees, buyer's remorse. They don't define you unless you let them. Progress starts the moment you decide to learn instead of blame.

When old thoughts creep in, swap them for something better:

- Instead of *I'm bad with money*, try *I'm figuring it out.*
- Instead of *I'll never catch up*, try *I can make progress from where I am.*
- Instead of *Budgeting is punishment*, try *Budgeting creates options.*

The only thing that really keeps you broke is believing you can't change.

Finding Your Financial Why: Personalizing Your Money Goals

Most of us know we should save, but "should" doesn't get anyone excited. Your motivation has to be personal, something that makes you want to try, not something that makes you feel guilty. Everything gets easier when you know exactly what you want your money to do for you.

Think about the last time you felt genuinely excited about your future. Maybe it was planning a trip, picturing your first apartment, or finally paying off that one annoying bill. That feeling is your "why." It's the engine that keeps your financial car running when your motivation sputters.

Grab a piece of paper, or your phone's notes app, and list three things you want that cost money. It could be paying off tuition, saving for a move, or having enough to say yes to concert tickets without wincing. Writing it down makes it real.

The key is filtering out what you want from what everyone else thinks you should want. Just because your cousin is saving for a Tesla doesn't mean you have to. Maybe your dream purchase is a plane ticket, not a car payment. Money goals that come from you are the ones that are more likely to stick.

Two people might both have $500 saved, but for totally different reasons. One is helping family; the other is paying for a photography class. Both goals are valid. When your "why" is clear, it's easier to resist the random Amazon rabbit holes.

I've seen firsthand how having a clear purpose changes everything. One friend worked two jobs in college because she wanted her own place. The thought of waking up in an apartment she decorated herself kept her going through those late-night shifts. Another friend set aside $20 a week to help pay for his sister's textbooks. He didn't have much extra, but his "why" made every small sacrifice feel worth it. These stories aren't rare. Ask anyone who sticks with a budget or savings plan, and you'll always find a real reason behind it.

Here's a simple plan: Pick one mini-goal and start today. Save $100 for emergencies, tickets, or just peace of mind. Write it somewhere visible. Divide the total by how many weeks you have. If it's $100 in 5 weeks, that's 20 dollars a week, roughly one less takeout meal. Small math, big impact.

When motivation fades, and it will, picture the payoff. Think freedom, not fear. Your "why" is your anchor when things get messy.

FOMO, YOLO, and the Psychology of Smart Spending

Your phone has more influence over your wallet than you probably realize. One minute you're just scrolling, and the next you're convincing yourself that those sneakers, that weekend trip, or that new phone case will definitely change your life. It's not magic; it's marketing. You're being hit with hundreds of ads and "highlight reel" posts every day, and your brain is basically under constant financial peer pressure.

That pressure has two main flavors: FOMO (fear of missing out) and YOLO (you only live once). FOMO whispers that everyone else is out living their best lives while you're stuck budgeting. YOLO chimes in with "treat yourself," because hey, you work hard, right? Together, they make a perfect storm that pushes you toward quick decisions instead of smart ones.

Social media amplifies all of it. You scroll through pictures of beach vacations, upgraded cars, and perfectly curated apartments and think, *Wow, everyone's thriving except me.* But remember: People post their best 10% and crop out the other 90. You don't see the credit card bills, the payment plans, or the stress behind those perfect smiles. It's easy to compare your real life to someone else's highlight reel and feel behind. But you're not behind; you're just comparing full reality to a filtered moment.

Emotions play a huge role in spending. Retail therapy gives a quick rush, especially after a tough day or when you're bored and looking for a distraction. That little "add to cart" dopamine hit feels good, but it fades fast, leaving you with guilt and a smaller balance. It's not a moral failure; it's biology. Companies spend billions designing websites and ads that make your brain crave that quick reward. Don't beat yourself up over falling for it. You're human.

How to Break the Spending Cycle

To start breaking the cycle, give yourself a pause button. The *24-hour rule* is simple but powerful. If you see something you want, wait a day before buying. Most of the time, the excitement fades, and you realize you didn't really need it. If you're still thinking about it the next day and it fits your budget, then go for it. That one small habit can save you hundreds over time.

Another trick is keeping a quick *spending journal*. You don't have to track every coffee or snack, but jot down what you bought, when, and what mood you were in. You'll start to see patterns: Maybe you overspend when you're stressed, tired, or just bored. Once you spot those triggers, you can replace them with something that doesn't drain your account, like a walk, a playlist, or a chat with a friend.

Before hitting "Add to Cart," ask yourself a few grounding questions:

- Do I actually need this, or is this just boredom in disguise?
- Am I buying this to feel better, or to look better online?
- Will I still care about this next week?
- Can I afford it without dipping in to money for bills or goals?

- What will I have to give up later if I spend this now?

If you can't answer those comfortably, it's a good sign to wait. Smart spending means choosing moments that actually matter. You can still treat yourself sometimes if you are smart about it.

FOMO also shows up socially. You get invited to dinner, a concert, or a weekend getaway that sounds fun but will wreck your budget. Saying no feels like social exile, especially when photos of the event flood your feed later. But the truth is that the people who matter won't care if you skip a few outings to stay financially grounded. Real friends understand. And if they don't, that's useful information, too.

Saying no gets easier with practice. You don't have to deliver a dramatic speech about your budget. Just keep it simple and confident.

Money Boundaries for Real Life: Possible Responses

- "That looks awesome, but I'm saving for something big right now."
- "I'd love to hang out, but I'm keeping it low-key this week. Let's plan something cheaper."
- "I'm skipping this one to stay on track, and next time's on me."

These responses keep your boundaries clear without killing the vibe. You're still showing up socially, just on your terms.

Intentional spending means matching your money with your values, not your impulses. If something truly adds joy to your life, go for it, even if it's small. A $20 meal with friends that fills you up emotionally is worth more than a $200 splurge you'll forget about next week. But if a purchase only adds stress or comparison, it's not a bargain at any price.

Remember that you're not boring for being responsible. You're not "missing out" because you chose peace of mind over pressure. Every time you pause before spending, you're building a habit that strengthens your confidence. And when FOMO hits again, because it will, you'll know how to handle it without letting your debit card do gymnastics.

From "Bad With Money" to Money Pro: Building Financial Confidence Fast

Let's be honest: Nobody is naturally "good" with money. Confidence isn't something you're born with; it's something you build, one small win at a time. Think of it like learning to cook. The first few tries might be messy, but the more you practice, the easier it gets. Money works the same way.

Financial confidence grows through repetition, not perfection. Checking your balance, paying a bill on time, or transferring a few dollars into savings may not feel like much, but every small action chips away at fear and builds familiarity. Over time, those little steps turn into habits, and habits create confidence.

Everyone has a "What was I thinking?" money story. Maybe you spent your first paycheck celebrating the fact that you got one, or forgot to cancel a subscription that quietly drained your account. That doesn't make you bad with money; it makes you human. The important part is to learn, adjust, and move forward instead of letting one mistake define you.

Start simple. Open a savings account, even if you only add five dollars. Look up your credit score just to know where you stand. Download a budgeting app and explore how it works. You don't need to do everything at once; you just need to begin. Each small action is proof that you can handle your finances.

If motivation helps, turn it into a game. Keep a checklist or tracker and give yourself credit for every "money win": paying a bill early, cooking instead of ordering out, or canceling a forgotten subscription. Those little victories retrain your brain to see money as progress, not pressure.

Confidence also comes from problem-solving. Maybe you can call the phone company about an overcharge and save money just by asking. Or use a rent-splitting app to end roommate drama. These moments are small choices that build real skills.

And when mistakes happen, don't spiral. Missed payments and over-drafts aren't disasters; they're lessons. The people who seem confident with money have made the same blunders; they just fixed them and moved on. Your financial story might have failures, but you can get up faster each time and be better for it.

Money Mastery Micro-Challenge

Try this one-week tracker:

- **Day 1:** Check your account balance.
- **Day 2:** Move five dollars into savings (or whatever amount you can).
- **Day 3:** Look up your credit score.
- **Day 4:** Download and open a budgeting app.
- **Day 5:** Cancel an unused subscription.
- **Day 6:** Set an alert for low balances or bills.
- **Day 7:** Talk to a friend about money. Split a bill or share one new trick.

Check each one off. Watch your confidence grow faster than your feed refreshes. Nobody expects perfection, just progress. Each tiny step proves you are leveling up. Keep going. Your next win is closer than you think.

Now that you've started shifting your mindset and building a little money confidence, it's time to get your financial house in order. You've learned that managing money requires taking real-world steps that make life smoother. The first step? Opening a bank account that actually works for you.

Chapter 2

Getting Your Financial House in Order

Banking, Paychecks, and Digital Basics

You've started shifting how you think about money, and now it's time to take action. This chapter will help you put your financial basics in order so that daily life runs smoothly. You'll learn how to open a bank account, read a paycheck, use modern apps, avoid fees, and protect your money online. Once these foundations are in place, everything else about personal finance gets easier.

How to Open Your First Bank Account (And Actually Use It)

You just got your first real paycheck and need a safe place to keep it. A bank account is your launchpad into adult life. It's how you get paid, pay friends, and finally move beyond loose cash and IOUs. With so many banks claiming to be "the best," though, it can be tough to know where to start. Should you walk into a local branch or open an online account from your couch in your pajamas? Either way, you're making a smart move by giving your money a real home (pajamas optional).

You have two main options: traditional banks and online banks.

- **Traditional banks** (like Wells Fargo, Chase, or Bank of America) have physical branches, real people to talk to, and easier cash deposits.

- **Online banks** (like Chime, SoFi, Ally, or Capital One 360) usually offer higher interest rates, fewer fees, and apps designed for mobile living.

There's no single right answer. If you prefer personal help and handle cash often, go traditional. If you value convenience and low fees, online banking may be the better fit.

Before opening an account, check the details. Not every "free checking" account is truly free. Look for:

- No monthly maintenance fees
- No minimum balance requirement
- Free access to ATMs (Allpoint or MoneyPass networks help you dodge those $2–5 withdrawal fees)
- A reliable mobile app that lets you check balances, deposit checks, and lock your card if needed

Simple Checking Account Fee Comparison*

Bank Name	Monthly Fee	Min Deposit	Free ATMs	Overdraft Policy
Chime	$0	$0	60k (Allpoint)	No fees; SpotMe covers up to $200
Ally Bank	$0	$0	43k (Allpoint)	Declines transactions; no overdraft fees
SoFi Bank	$0	$0	55k (Allpoint)	No overdraft fees for eligible accounts
Capital One 360	$0	$0	70k (Capital One, Allpoint, MoneyPass)	Free coverage up to $200; otherwise declines
Alliant Credit Union (example)	$2	$2	80k (Allpoint)	No fees; optional overdraft protection
Big Bank USA (example)	$12	$25	16k+	$30+ per overdraft

Data as of Dec 2025

To open the account, bring a government-issued ID, your Social Security number, and proof of address. Some banks require a small deposit, while others let you start with nothing. You'll usually get a debit card within a week, or instantly if you open the account in person.

Now That You've Opened an Account

Once your account is open, start by making it secure. Choose a strong password that mixes letters, numbers, and symbols that a hacker couldn't guess by scrolling through your social media. Avoid using your birthday, pet's name, or the word "money." If your bank offers two-factor authentication, turn it on. That extra verification step, like a code sent to your phone, keeps your account safe even if someone figures out your password.

Next, set up direct deposit so your paycheck goes straight into your account. It's faster, safer, and more reliable than waiting for paper checks. Some banks even let you access your pay early, which is great if payday always feels too far away. The less time your money spends floating around, the better.

After that, use your account for online bill payments instead of mailing checks or juggling multiple apps. Most banks let you schedule or automate recurring payments like rent, phone, or insurance. Automation helps you stay organized; just make sure the money is there before payments pull.

Make a habit of checking your balance weekly (or more often, if you're getting into the groove). A quick glance helps catch double charges, late fees, or forgotten subscriptions before they cause trouble. Turn on alerts for low balances or large transactions so you'll know right away if something unusual happens.

Think of your checking account as your "daily wallet," where income comes in, and expenses go out. Your savings account is your "safety stash," reserved for emergencies, big purchases, or future goals. Keeping them separate helps you avoid that "I thought I had more" moment when bills hit.

Once everything is in place, you'll feel more in control of not only your bank account but your entire financial life. Security, organization, and a few smart habits can turn your account from a source of stress into a steady foundation.

Decoding Your Paycheck: What Every Line Means

Your first paycheck hits your account, and for a brief, shining moment, you feel rich. Then you look closer at the stub and realize a chunk of your money has mysteriously disappeared. Don't panic. That's not your boss shortchanging you; it's just how taxes and deductions work. I remember getting my first real paycheck and thinking, *Who took half my money?* It turned out to be the government, not a thief, but it still stung.

Let's break it down so you actually know where every dollar goes.

Your gross pay is the big number at the top, the total amount you earned before any deductions. That's what you'd make in a world without taxes or health insurance, otherwise known as a fantasy. It's nice to look at, but don't plan your weekend around it.

Next come the deductions, which are the legitimate reasons your check is smaller:

- **Federal and state taxes:** These are based on how much you make, where you live, and what you entered on your W-4 form when you started the job. That form tells your employer how much to withhold for income taxes. Fill it out carefully; too little withheld and you'll owe at tax time, too much and you've just given the government an interest-free loan.
- **FICA taxes:** These include Social Security (6.2%) and Medicare (1.45%), combined under the *Federal Insurance Contributions Act* (*FICA*). You could see them listed together on your pay stub. They fund programs that support retirees and people with disabilities, so think of it as helping your future self and everyone's grandma.

- **Insurance premiums or retirement contributions:** If your job offers benefits like health insurance, an HSA, or a 401(k), you'll see those listed here. They lower your paycheck now, but save you from financial headaches later. Think of them as "grown-up safety features."

Your stub might also show other items like union dues, charitable contributions, or pretax commuter benefits, if your employer offers them. Every line tells part of your financial story, so don't just skim it. Understanding your deductions helps you make smarter choices.

Sample Pay Check

		Current			YTD	
	Hours/Units	Rate	Amount	Hours/Units	Amount	
Earnings	80.0000		**$3,393.46**	1,200.0000	**$56,601.75**	
Regular	80.0000	42.4183	$3,393.46	1,080.0000	$45,811.71	
Paid Time Off				64.0000	$2,714.76	
Holiday				56.0000	$2,375.43	
Seasonal Bonus					$5,699.85	
Taxable Benefits			**$8.39**		**$117.46**	
Group Term Life			$8.39		$117.46	
Memo Information			**$122.63**		**$1,989.62**	
HSA ER			$20.83		$291.62	
401K Roth ER			$101.80		$1,698.00	
Pre-Tax Deductions			**$142.85**		**$1,999.90**	
Dental Pretax			$11.83		$165.62	
Med Pretax			$106.53		$1,491.42	
Vision Pretax			$3.66		$51.24	
HSA Self			$20.83		$291.62	
Taxes			**$650.65**		**$11,491.37**	
Federal			$401.33		$7,305.34	
Social Security			$202.06		$3,392.60	
Medicare			$47.26		$793.43	
Post-Tax Deductions			**$302.75**		**$4,965.97**	
Critical Illnes			$18.50		$259.00	
401K ROTH			$271.48		$4,528.19	
Group Accident			$2.69		$37.66	
Hospital			$10.08		$141.12	
			Amount		**Amount**	
Net Pay			**$2,297.21**		**$38,144.51**	

- **Gross pay:** $3,393.46
- **Federal tax:** −$401.33
- **State tax:** −$0
- **FICA (Social Security + Medicare):** −$249.32
- **Health insurance (dental, medical, vision):** − $122.02
- **HSA (health savings account):** −$20.83

- **Retirement:** –$271.48
- **Other deductions (hospital, group accident, critical illness):** –$31.27
- **Net pay:** $2,297.21

That final number, net pay, is what you actually take home. It's the number that shows up in your bank account, the one that decides whether you're eating sushi or instant noodles this week.

If your take-home pay ever seems off, don't ignore it. Check your hours, pay rate, and deductions line by line. Sometimes, a missed overtime entry or a wrong withholding setting can throw things off. Payroll systems are run by humans (using software built by humans), so mistakes happen. Catching one early can save you a major headache later. If something doesn't look right, talk to HR or payroll. You're being smart, and it's worth the hassle.

It's also worth double-checking your W-4 form once in a while, especially if you pick up a side job, get married, or your income changes. You can update it anytime to fine-tune how much gets withheld. Think of it as adjusting the thermostat on your taxes. A small tweak can keep things comfortable when April rolls around.

Direct deposit is still the easiest and safest way to get paid. No paper checks to lose and no awkward bank lines on Friday afternoon. You can even split your deposit between two accounts to save automatically. For instance, send most of it to checking for bills and daily expenses and route a smaller portion directly into savings. It's like paying your future self before you pay anyone else. If your bank allows early access to direct deposits, that's even better. There's nothing like payday arriving a day early to make you feel like you've cracked the system.

Once you understand how your paycheck works, the mystery fades fast. You'll see where your money really goes, how to spot errors, and how to plan around your take-home pay. That confidence makes payday feel more rewarding and might even stop you from refreshing your banking app every five minutes, wondering where it all went. Remember, the goal isn't just to get paid; it's to know what your money is doing once it lands in your account.

Quick Guide: Benefits and Insurance Starter Pack

Now that you know where your paycheck is going, let's look at what those deductions do for you. Those acronyms like HSA, FSA, 401(k), and PPO are not random; they are part of your total compensation. Understanding them helps you use your job benefits to your advantage instead of letting them go unused.

Health Insurance

- **Premium:** What you pay each month to stay covered
- **Deductible:** What you pay out of pocket before insurance starts helping
- **Copay:** A flat fee for visits, such as $25 for a doctor's appointment
- **Out-of-pocket max:** The most you will pay in a year before insurance covers 100%

If you are healthy and rarely see a doctor, a high-deductible health plan (HDHP) with a health savings account (HSA) can save you money. You will pay lower premiums, and the HSA lets you set aside tax-free money for future medical expenses. The best part is that HSA funds roll over every year and grow with interest.

FSA vs. HSA (The Quick Fix for Confusion)

- **FSA (flexible spending account):** Use it within the year, as most funds do not roll over.

- **HSA (health savings account):** Stays with you and rolls over annually.

PPO vs. HMO

- **PPO (preferred provider organization):** Offers more flexibility in choosing doctors and specialists without needing referrals, but premiums are usually higher.
- **HMO (health maintenance organization):** Requires you to choose a primary doctor within a certain network and get referrals for specialists, but premiums are often lower.

401(k) and Retirement Contributions

A 401(k) is an employer-sponsored retirement account that lets you set aside part of your paycheck before taxes. Many employers offer a matching contribution, which is essentially free money for your future. Always contribute enough to get the full match if it's offered.

Dental and Vision Insurance

These are usually low-cost add-ons that cover cleanings, checkups, glasses, and contact lenses. Skipping them can end up costing more later.

Disability and Life Insurance

- **Disability insurance:** Replaces part of your income if you cannot work due to injury or illness.
- **Life insurance:** Not essential yet unless others depend on your income, but good to understand for the future.

Understanding your benefits is more than knowing what gets deducted from your paycheck. You need to recognize how each program protects your health, builds your safety net, and shapes your financial stability. Once your paycheck and benefits are set up, the next step is learning how to manage your money day-to-day through modern tools and technology. Let's look at how mobile banking and fintech apps can make handling your finances easier, faster, and smarter.

Mastering Mobile Banking: Choosing the Right Fintech Apps

Once upon a time, "banking" meant standing in line at a branch on your lunch break, waiting to deposit a paper check. Today, your bank lives in your pocket. You can check your balance in seconds, transfer money to friends, or set savings goals before your coffee gets cold. Mobile banking and fintech apps have turned managing money into something you can actually do anywhere, even from the comfort of your couch.

There are hundreds of apps out there, but not all are created equal. Some are built for budgeting, some for investing, and others for simplifying your daily transactions. Let's sort through what you really need so your phone becomes your personal financial control center.

Before you dive into specific fintech tools, make sure your main bank's app checks all the right boxes. A solid banking app should make your life easier, safer, and more efficient. Here's what to look for:

Checklist: What Do I Need From My Bank App?

- Mobile check deposit
- No monthly fees
- Free ATMs nearby

- Top-notch security (biometrics, 2FA)
- Simple, clean interface
- Budgeting and savings tools
- Peer payment integration (Venmo, Cash App)
- Responsive customer support

If your app doesn't offer most of these features, you might be missing out on convenience, protection, and peace of mind. When I opened my first online account, I remember thinking, *How different can apps really be?* Then I learned the hard way that one missing alert can lead to an overdraft fee. Choose your main banking app like you'd choose a car: It should be reliable, efficient, and built to protect you.

Budgeting Apps: Know Where It's All Going

If you've ever wondered, *Where did all my money go?*, these apps have your answer. Budgeting apps track your spending automatically by connecting to your accounts and categorizing purchases.

Popular options include Rocket Money, YNAB (You Need a Budget), EveryDollar, and PocketGuard. Rocket Money helps you spot and cancel unused subscriptions before they drain your wallet. YNAB teaches you to assign every dollar a job so your money works for you instead of disappearing midweek. EveryDollar is perfect for zero-based budgeting, while PocketGuard gives you a quick view of how much "safe to spend" money you have left.

When I first started using a budgeting app, I was shocked by how often I tapped "Confirm" on fast-food orders. Seeing it in black and white was humbling but motivating. That's the power of awareness.

Try a few and see which one fits your style. Think of it like picking a workout plan. They all help you get financially fit, but each one has its own routine.

Payment Apps: Send, Split, and Settle Up

No more awkward IOUs or "I'll Venmo you later" that never happens. Payment apps make splitting bills and paying friends painless.

The big names are Venmo, Cash App, PayPal, and Zelle. Venmo keeps things social, Cash App lets you invest and use a debit card, PayPal is the long-standing, all-purpose platform that works anywhere, and Zelle moves money directly between banks with no waiting.

Just remember that these are payment tools, not savings accounts. Don't store large balances in them for long. Once the money lands, move it back to your bank. Also, double-check who you're paying before you hit "Send." One wrong username and your roommate's rent money could end up with a stranger named "V3nmoKing."

Savings and Investing Apps: Grow What You've Got

If you've ever thought, *I'll start investing someday*, that day can be today. Modern fintech apps make it simple to begin with just a few dollars.

Apps like SoFi and Acorns can help you invest small amounts automatically. Acorns rounds up your everyday purchases and invests the spare change. SoFi offers beginner-friendly investment accounts, goal tracking, and even free educational content. It's never been easier to dip your toes into investing without fancy suits or confusing stock charts.

And if you're not ready to invest yet, start small with an automatic savings app. Many banks now let you set "round-up" rules, moving spare change from each purchase straight into your savings. It's passive progress that adds up over time.

Safety First: Protecting Your Digital Wallet

With great convenience comes great responsibility. Always download apps from trusted sources such as the Apple App Store or Google Play, and stick with established financial brands. Avoid anything promising instant wealth or guaranteed returns. If it sounds too good to be true, it probably is.

Set up two-factor authentication (2FA) on your banking and payment apps. That extra login code might feel inconvenient, but it can stop hackers in their tracks. If you lose your phone, use your bank's app or website to lock your card immediately. Public Wi-Fi is another risk, so avoid logging into financial apps while sitting in a coffee shop or airport. Your vanilla latte isn't worth the chance of a stolen password.

Find Your Perfect Combo

You don't need 10 apps to manage your money. The best setup is simple and fits your lifestyle. You might use a budgeting app to track spending, a payment app to split bills, and your bank's app for checking balances. That's plenty.

Test, compare, and delete the ones you don't need. Streamlining your financial life keeps you focused and makes managing money feel less like a chore. Once you find the right mix, you'll realize that financial control isn't complicated and keeps you organized.

Avoiding Overdrafts, Fees, and Sneaky Charges

Few things are more of a buzzkill than checking your account and spotting a random fee you didn't expect. Maybe it's a $35 overdraft fee from buying coffee when your balance was low, or a $2.50 charge for using a "foreign" ATM two blocks away. These little hits might seem harmless at first, but they add up fast, and banks know it. Every year, they make billions off customers who don't notice small fees quietly nibbling away at their balance.

If you ever look closely at your bank statement, you'll probably see terms like "Monthly Maintenance Fee," "Overdraft Fee," "ATM Surcharge," or "Foreign Transaction Fee." Each one has its own fine print, but the end result is the same: less money in your pocket. Understanding how these charges work is the first step to stopping them.

The Most Common Fees

The most common culprits are overdraft fees, maintenance fees, and ATM charges. Overdraft fees happen when your balance drops below zero, even by a few dollars. Monthly maintenance fees appear if you don't meet minimum balance or direct deposit requirements. And ATM fees? Those can hit twice—once from your bank and again from the ATM owner. There are also paper statement fees, foreign transaction charges when you shop online from overseas retailers, and even inactivity fees for accounts that sit idle too long.

The good news is that most of these can be avoided with a few smart habits.

Start by turning on low-balance alerts in your banking app. Almost every bank offers them now. Set yours to notify you when your account dips below an amount you choose—maybe $50 or $100—so you get a heads-up before your next purchase puts you in the red. I once got saved by one of these alerts right before a rent payment hit. Without it, I would have been staring at a negative balance for days.

Next, always watch your available balance, not just your "current balance." Pending transactions, like that weekend takeout or a gas station hold, might not show up right away. That delay can make you think you have more money than you actually do. I made that mistake early on and ended up overdrafting because a small payment took longer to clear. A quick daily glance at your app can help you avoid that trap completely.

Stick to your bank's fee-free ATM network. Using another bank's machine can cost anywhere from $2 to $5 per withdrawal, and both banks can charge you. Most banking apps show a map of free ATMs nearby. It takes an extra 30 seconds to check, and that's money you get to keep.

If you're constantly bumping into fees, it might be time to switch accounts. Many online banks and credit unions now offer checking accounts with no overdraft or monthly maintenance fees. Some even let you link your savings account as overdraft protection, automatically transferring money if your checking balance drops too low. If you're a student, ask about student accounts that often come with built-in fee waivers.

Occasionally, mistakes happen, like a bill hitting early or a subscription renewing before payday. If you get charged a fee, call your bank's customer service and politely ask if they'll waive it. A simple, "Hi, I noticed an overdraft fee. This is my first time. Could it be reversed as a courtesy?" often works. I've done this myself, and more often than not, they removed the charge right away. Banks would rather keep a good customer than lose one over a single fee.

Watch out for sneaky charges, too. Some foreign websites add a hidden 1–3% fee for transactions processed outside the US, even if prices are listed in dollars. And always double-check those $0.99 "trial" subscriptions. Many quietly turn into full-priced renewals after 30 days. I once got charged for a streaming app I didn't even remember signing up for. Now, I keep a short list of all my subscriptions in my phone's notes app and review it once a month.

Maintenance fees can also creep up if your account falls below a set balance or doesn't get enough deposits each month. Avoid them by opting for electronic statements, setting up direct deposit, or choosing a no-minimum-balance account. Spending 10 minutes comparing bank policies could easily save you hundreds of dollars a year.

If you're curious where your money is really leaking, grab a recent bank statement and highlight every word that says "fee" or "charge." You'll quickly see patterns, whether it's frequent ATM use, over-drafts, or monthly service costs. From there, find ways to eliminate them. Switching banks is easier than ever, and there are plenty of fee-free options, including Chime, SoFi, and Capital One 360.

The bottom line? Staying alert pays off, literally. A few small habits like setting alerts, reviewing your statements, and asking for refunds when fees sneak in can protect your balance and give you a sense of control. Banks count on customers not paying attention. Once you start paying attention, you flip the script.

You've worked hard for your money. Keep it that way.

Traditional Banks vs. Credit Unions vs. Online Banks			
Feature	Traditional Banks	Credit Unions	Online Banks
Monthly Fees	Common; usually $5-$15 unless requirements are met	Rare; many accounts are free	Usually None
Minimum Balance	Often required	Low or none	Low or none
Overdraft Fees	Typically $25-$35	Lower; sometimes $10-$15	Low or none; some decline instead of charging
ATM Access / Fees	Strong network but out-of-network fees common	Big shared networks with many free ATMs	Large partner networks; minimal fees if in-network
Interest Rates	Usually low	Often better	Often the highest
Digital Experience	Strong apps	Good apps (varies)	Excellent; mobile-first
Eligibility	Anyone	Must meet membership criteria	Anyone

Digital Security 101: Protecting Your Cash From Scams

You can have the best banking app, the slickest budget tracker, and a growing savings balance, but if your security game is weak, you're still at risk. Scammers today aren't hiding in dark corners of the internet; they are sliding into inboxes, texting from fake "bank numbers," and even calling with convincing voices that sound like they've worked at your branch for years. Their goal is simple: to trick you into handing over passwords, money, or personal info.

I remember the first time I got a text saying my "account was locked" with a link to fix it. It looked official, complete with the bank logo and urgent wording. I almost tapped it until I noticed one small typo in the web address. That tiny detail saved me a huge headache. It probably also saved me a week of explaining to customer service why I sent my info to "bank-secure-verify.biz."

Scammers thrive on emotion such as panic, curiosity, or guilt. If a message ever makes you feel rushed or pressured, that's your first red flag. Legitimate banks will never ask for your password, PIN, or full Social Security number through text or email. When in doubt, call your bank directly using the number on your card, not the one in the message.

Spotting the Red Flags

Here's how to recognize scams before they strike:

- **Phishing emails:** Fake messages pretending to be from your bank or a trusted company. Hover over links before clicking. If the address looks strange or misspelled, delete it immediately.
- **Smishing (text scams):** Texts that say "Your account is locked" or "Unusual activity detected." Don't reply, and definitely don't click the link. Just delete the message and move on with your day.
- **Vishing (voice scams):** Calls from people pretending to be from your bank's "fraud department." They may ask you to verify account details or codes. Hang up and call your bank directly. The real fraud department will not be offended.

- **Fake shopping sites:** If an online deal looks too good to be true, it probably is. That $10 pair of AirPods? Fake. Always look for "https" in the website address and read a few reviews before entering payment info.

Your best defense is simple: Pause before you click. That extra second can save you hundreds of dollars and a few new gray hairs.

Passwords, Passkeys, and Two-Factor Protection

Think of your password like the key to your front door. If someone else gets it, they can walk right in and eat your snacks. Avoid easy ones like your birthday, "password123," or your pet's name (especially if your Instagram bio says "Dog Mom to Max"). Instead, use long, unique combinations of letters, numbers, and symbols. And please, don't reuse the same password across multiple sites. Once a hacker has one, they will test it everywhere.

If that sounds overwhelming, use a password manager, which is like a secure vault for your login information. It stores all your usernames and passwords in an encrypted database that only you can unlock with one master password. You can also use it to generate strong, random passwords that are nearly impossible to guess. Unlike saving passwords in your browser or phone notes, which is like hiding your house key under the doormat, password managers keep your credentials locked up tight even if your device gets hacked.

Popular, trusted options include 1Password, Bitwarden, and Dashlane. They sync across your phone and computer, autofill passwords on legitimate sites, and remind you to update weak or reused ones. Once you set one up, you will wonder how you ever lived without it. Your future self will thank you for not using "MaxTheDog2024!" for every login.

You will also start seeing a newer, more secure option called passkeys. Passkeys replace traditional passwords with a fingerprint, face scan, or device PIN. They are safer because they cannot be guessed or stolen through phishing. Many major banks, Google, Apple, and PayPal now support passkeys. I set one up for my bank last year, and I love it. It is faster, easier, and far less stressful than trying to remember which version of your password has the exclamation point at the end.

On top of that, always turn on two-factor authentication (2FA). This adds an extra layer of security, usually by sending a code to your phone or email before logging in. It might feel like an extra step, but it is one of the easiest ways to stop hackers cold. Even if they get your password, they cannot get in without that second code.

Safe Browsing and Secure Networks

Avoid logging in to financial apps while connected to public Wi-Fi at coffee shops, airports, or libraries. Those networks are wide open to hackers, and trust me, you do not want to make their day easier. If you have to use one, connect through a VPN (Virtual Private Network) to encrypt your data.

Keep your phone and apps updated, too. Those updates you ignore often include vital security fixes. The five minutes it takes to update could save you a massive headache later.

And when you are done banking, always log out. It sounds obvious, but leaving your account open is like walking away from an ATM without taking your card.

Stay Alert and Respond Fast

Even with good habits, it is smart to check your accounts regularly. Turn on transaction alerts so you know every time money leaves your account. Review your statements weekly and act fast if you spot anything strange. Banks can usually reverse fraudulent charges quickly if you catch them early.

Keep a secure backup of important financial info, like account numbers and contact details. You can store it printed and locked away, or saved in an encrypted file. That way, if your phone is lost or hacked, you are not scrambling to recover everything.

The Real-World Takeaway

Digital safety is all about being prepared. It might sound paranoid, but the truth is that scammers are always inventing new tricks, so stay one step ahead by using password managers and passkeys, questioning anything that feels off, and checking your accounts often.

Think of it like locking your doors at night. You do not do it because you expect trouble; you do it because it is smart. The same logic applies online. A few extra steps of caution today can save you a lot of explaining to your bank later. Protect your digital money like you protect your pizza delivery tracker, because both deserve your attention.

Now that your money is safe, your apps are secure, and you've got a handle on avoiding sneaky fees, it's time to take the next step: deciding what to do with your cash once it's in your account. In the next chapter, we'll shift gears from protection to planning. You'll learn how to create a budget that's realistic, flexible, and totally doable, no matter what your income looks like. No complicated spreadsheets or math headaches (unless that's your thing), just a simple system that helps you tell your money where to go instead of wondering where it went.

Chapter 3

Real-Life Budgeting That Works

Zero-Based Budgeting for When Every Dollar Counts

You know that slightly sick feeling you get when you check your balance the day before payday and wonder where all your money went? It's like searching for socks in the dryer; somehow, they just vanish. That's where zero-based budgeting steps in to save the day. Instead of hoping you have something left at the end of the month, you tell every single dollar where to go before you spend it. No more mystery money disappearing on snacks or random Amazon "necessities." With zero-based budgeting, if you earn $1,200 this month, you assign every penny a job until there's nothing left unaccounted for. It's perfect for anyone tired of guessing where their cash went or pretending "pending transactions" are invisible.

The beauty of this system is that it is intentional. You plan for rent and groceries, sure, but you also include the small stuff, like your Spotify bill, your caffeine habit, and that "I deserve it" Friday-night burrito. When everything is written down, there's no more wondering why your account balance suddenly looks like tumbleweeds.

Getting Started

Start by listing your total income for the month. That means every-thing: your job, side gigs, cash tips, and even the random ten dollars your friend Venmoed you for pizza. Then list your expenses. Split them into fixed costs, such as rent, your phone bill, or subscriptions, and variable ones like groceries, gas, snacks, and fun money. The goal is simple: income minus expenses equals zero. That doesn't mean you empty your bank account. It means every dollar has a destination, whether it's going toward bills, savings, or paying off a little debt.

Let's walk through a quick example. Say you make $1,200 from your retail job, DoorDash runs, and a bit of tutoring. Write that total at the top of your sheet. Next, break down your expenses: rent ($500), phone bill ($60), groceries ($200), streaming ($30), transportation ($70), and fun money ($80). Don't forget sneaky things like toiletries or laundry soap; they add up faster than you'd think. Save at least a little, even if it's just $30. If your totals don't balance, adjust. Maybe skip one takeout order or hold off on that impulse hoodie. If you find extra money left, throw it into savings or toward debt so every dollar has a purpose.

If your income changes from week to week, this method becomes your secret weapon. Figure out your lowest-income month and base your plan on that. When you earn more, don't celebrate by panic-adding things to your cart. Assign the extra immediately to savings or goals. That way, high weeks feel like progress instead of "oops, where did it all go?"

When I first tried zero-based budgeting, I was skeptical. It felt like too much work until I realized how good it feels to know where my money is going. There's something weirdly satisfying about watching your plan add up and seeing those mystery expenses disappear. Plus, I stopped having that mini–heart attack every time I swiped my card and prayed it would go through.

Build yourself a bare-bones budget for the rough patches. This is your survival plan for lean months. List only the must-haves, such as rent, food, and your phone bill, and total them up. Knowing that number gives you peace of mind. If your income drops, you can switch to that plan right away instead of spiraling. Think of it like a financial safety net, just without the trampoline.

Plug-and-Play Zero-Based Budgeting Template

Here's what a zero-based budget looks like in action. You can build it in a notebook, a spreadsheet, or any app that tracks income and expenses:

Income Sources	Amount
Retail Job	$800
DoorDash	$250
Tutoring	$150
Total Income	**$1,200**

Expense	Amount
Rent	$500
Groceries	$200
Phone Bill	$60
Streaming Services	$30
Transportation	$70
Fun Money	$80
Laundry/Toiletries	$30
School Fees	$20
Savings/Emergency	$30
Total Expenses	**$1,020**
Surplus (+) / Deficit (-)	**$180**

In this example, total income is $1,200 and total expenses are $1,020, leaving $180 unassigned. That leftover cash isn't bonus money. Give it a job right away. Move it into savings, pay down debt, or stash it in an emergency fund until income minus expenses equals zero.

If your expenses come out higher than your income, don't panic. This is where you make small changes. Maybe pause one streaming service, skip an extra night out, or meal-prep instead of ordering take-out. Tiny adjustments can balance things faster than you expect.

If your paychecks aren't steady, start with your bare-bones version and treat anything extra as gravy. Never rely on your high-earning weeks to cover your regular bills. When extra cash shows up, decide its purpose immediately. Savings, debt payoff, or even that wish-list item you've been eyeing all count, just make it intentional.

If you're a fan of digital tools, most budgeting apps can automate the process. You can create custom categories, color-code your spending, and set alerts when you're close to overspending. Some apps even let you auto-transfer leftover money into savings so you don't accidentally treat yourself before rent clears.

Successful zero-based budgeting requires paying careful attention to your finances. The more you practice, the more natural it feels. You'll start noticing patterns, spending smarter, and feeling more in control. It's one of the simplest ways to go from guessing to knowing and from stressed to steady.

50/30/20 and Beyond: Finding the Right Budget for Your Life

If zero-based budgeting feels a little too hands-on for your style, the 50/30/20 rule might be your ideal starting point. It's simple, forgiving, and doesn't require tracking every dollar with detective-level detail. You just divide your after-tax income into three easy chunks:

50% for needs, 30% for wants, and 20% for savings or debt payoff. That's it. No complicated math or color-coded spreadsheets required.

Needs are the non-negotiables like rent, groceries, utilities, transportation, and minimum loan payments. Wants are your fun stuff, such as takeout, travel, new clothes, or that concert ticket you swore was a "one-time splurge." Savings and debt go toward your future self: emergency funds, investments, or paying off credit cards.

Picture your paycheck like a pizza. Half keeps you alive, about a third makes life worth living, and the last slice helps your future self breathe a little easier. But be honest. Don't pretend your sushi habit is a grocery need. It's a want, and that's okay.

Now, real life doesn't always fit these perfect percentages. Maybe your rent takes up 60% of your income because you live in an expensive area. Or maybe you're in debt-busting mode and want to throw 30% toward paying it down. That's fine. The 50/30/20 rule isn't a strict formula. It's a flexible framework you can bend to your situation without feeling like you broke the rules.

When I first tried this system, I discovered that "coffee runs" were eating more of my budget than I thought. Once I saw it laid out, I had to laugh (and maybe cringe a little). It showed me what was quietly eating my money.

Other Savings Methods

If you prefer something more visual, the envelope method is a classic. Label envelopes for groceries, gas, or entertainment, and stuff them with cash at the start of the month. Once an envelope is empty, that's it—you stop spending from that category. It's oddly satisfying and humbling at the same time.

If you prefer automation, the pay-yourself-first method makes saving effortless. The second your paycheck hits, you move money into savings or debt payments before spending on anything else. You're basically paying your future self first and current you second. When I set up auto-transfers this way, it felt like a cheat code for adulting.

Each system has its strengths, so don't overthink it. Pick the one that fits your lifestyle and tweak it over time.

Here's a quick side-by-side comparison:

Method	Strengths	Weaknesses	Best For
50/30/20 Rule	Simple, flexible, low effort	Can feel too broad; tough in high-cost areas	Beginners and steady earners
Envelope Method	Visual and tactile; limits overspending	Less practical for card or app users	Cash users or those who overspend easily
Pay-Yourself-First	Automated savings; builds consistency	Can over-prioritize savings if not balanced	Impulse spenders or auto-deposit fans
Zero-Based Budgeting	Total control and detailed tracking	More time-consuming to maintain	Structure-lovers and detail-oriented users

Quick Summary:

- You can mix and match budgeting styles until one clicks.
- Zero-based means every dollar gets an assignment.
- The 50/30/20 rule gives you a balanced baseline, and you can adjust as needed.
- Budgeting apps make tracking less painful (and occasionally fun).

You'll also find downloadable budgeting spreadsheets in the Bonus Section at the back of the book. They're easy to use and ready for you to plug in your own numbers.

Apps That Help You Stay on Budget Without Losing Your Mind

- **Rocket Money** does more than just track spending. It automatically finds and cancels unwanted subscriptions, like that free trial you forgot about six months ago. It also gives you alerts when bills increase and can even help you negotiate lower rates on certain services.
- **Monarch Money** is perfect if you like to see everything in one place. It connects to your bank, credit cards, and investments, giving you a real-time picture of your finances and long-term goals. You can even share your dashboard with a partner or roommate to stay on the same page about money.
- **YNAB (You Need A Budget)** is for the detail-oriented crowd. It follows the "give every dollar a job" philosophy, meaning nothing goes unaccounted for. It takes a bit of effort to learn, but once you do, it feels incredibly empowering. You'll go from "I think I have enough" to "I know exactly where every penny is going."
- **EveryDollar**, created by Ramsey Solutions, offers a clean, drag-and-drop interface that's beginner-friendly. It's great for people who want something simple and visual without a steep learning curve. You can build your monthly plan in minutes and actually enjoy it, or at least not dread it.
- **Goodbudget** is the digital version of the envelope system. You divide your income into virtual envelopes for categories like food, entertainment, and transportation. Once an envelope is empty, you stop spending from that category. It's perfect if you like the control of cash but prefer to use your phone instead of carrying actual envelopes.
- **PocketGuard** is all about real-time control. It automatically calculates what's "safe to spend" after accounting for upcoming bills, savings goals, and essentials.

It's like having a money coach in your pocket saying, "Yes, you can get that latte," or "Maybe skip it because rent is due next week."

Comparison at a glance:

App	Best Feature	Drawbacks
Rocket Money	Auto-cancels subscriptions	Some features behind paywall
Monarch Money	Net worth and goal tracking	Monthly subscription fee
YNAB	Assigns every dollar a job	Steep learning curve
EveryDollar	Drag-and-adjust setup	Limited automation
Goodbudget	Digital envelope system	Manual entry required
PocketGuard	"Safe-to-spend"	Less customization

Take this quick quiz to see which system matches your personality:

Which Budget Are You?

1. What stresses you out most about money?
   a. Not knowing where it all goes
   b. Overspending without realizing it
   c. Forgetting to save
   d. Too many categories or steps
2. How do you get paid?
   a. Steady paycheck every two weeks
   b. Multiple gigs, never the same
   c. Direct deposit from one job
   d. Cash or apps from side hustles
3. Your favorite way to track things:
   a. Spreadsheets
   b. Cash or envelopes
   c. Automatic apps
   d. Pen and paper

4. What's your vibe when you sit down to look at your money?
    a. "Let me see exactly what's happening."
    b. "I like simple rules. Just tell me when I'm close to overspending."
    c. "I want everything automated so I don't forget."
    d. "I just need a quick overview, nothing too deep."
5. How do you react when you get unexpected extra money (like a bonus or refund)?
    a. I immediately assign it to categories or goals.
    b. I split it across envelopes or cash buckets.
    c. I send a chunk into savings before I spend anything.
    d. I treat myself first, then make sure my bills are fine.

Mostly a's: Try zero-based budgeting or YNAB for detailed control.

Mostly b's: The envelope method or Goodbudget will keep you accountable.

Mostly c's: Pay yourself first with an app like PocketGuard or Rocket Money.

Mostly d's: Use 50/30/20 or EveryDollar for simplicity.

Finding your budgeting style is all about momentum. Once you find one that clicks, you'll start to see real progress, less stress, and maybe even enjoy checking your balance for a change.

Budgeting With Roommates, Side Hustles, and Gig Work

Living with roommates is a whole new kind of budgeting adventure. Suddenly, rent is not just your problem, but a team effort filled with group chats, late Venmo reminders, and "who bought the toilet paper last time" debates. One missed payment and the vibe in the apartment can shift fast.

Maybe you have had that roommate who always forgets to Venmo for groceries or insists they will get it next time. Setting clear expectations early saves friendships and avoids awkward tension. Start by dividing big expenses such as rent, utilities, and Wi-Fi based on what is fair. Most people split things evenly, but if someone has the bigger room or uses the garage, talk about adjusting the amounts. It is easier to have one five-minute conversation than six months of silent resentment.

I learned this the hard way in my first apartment. My roommate and I assumed we would just "figure it out" as we went. Three months later, we were arguing over who owed what for cleaning supplies. After that, we sat down and created a shared spreadsheet. It took ten minutes, and it completely changed how we handled money from that point on.

Apps can help keep everyone sane. Splitwise is a lifesaver for tracking who owes what. You log shared bills or grocery trips, and the app does the math for you. Venmo and Cash App make it easy to pay each other back right away, while Zelle is great for rent or utilities because it connects directly to most bank accounts. Just remember that Zelle transfers usually cannot be canceled once sent, so double-check before tapping "Send."

You can try this system: Whenever someone covers a shared bill, snap a photo of the receipt and drop it into your group chat. Log it in Splitwise immediately so nothing gets lost. Set a recurring reminder in your phone to pay rent or utilities a few days before they are due. If someone is late, a friendly nudge like "Hey, rent is due Friday. Want me to remind you again Thursday night?" keeps it light but clear.

Sometimes you will need a roommate meeting to reset expectations. Keep it short and calm, maybe with snacks to lighten the mood. Saying "Hey, everyone, let's take five minutes to make sure we are good on bills" sounds way better than "You never pay me back." Small, honest talks beat months of quiet irritation every time.

If your household shares streaming services, subscriptions, or groceries, decide upfront who pays for what and when. Maybe one person covers Netflix and another handles Wi-Fi, or everyone pitches in for bulk groceries through a shared app. Writing it down once avoids a dozen "Didn't I pay last time?" arguments later.

Side Hustles and Other Income

Now, let's talk about side hustles and gig income. Maybe you deliver for Uber Eats on weekends, babysit for your neighbors, or sell custom sneakers online. Gig work can be unpredictable. One week, you are rolling in cash, and the next week, you hear crickets. That is why tracking income is key. Use a notes app or a Google Sheet to log every payment. Write down the date, source, and amount. At the end of each month, total it up so you know what you are earning.

If you juggle multiple gigs, consider using different columns or color codes to keep them organized. I once used a simple Google Sheet with tabs labeled "Tutoring," "Book Sales," and "Online Orders." Seeing the totals in one place helped me realize where my time was paying off and where it was not.

Self-employment also means no one is taking out taxes for you. A good rule of thumb is to set aside about 25–30% of your gig earnings in a separate account labeled "Taxes." It sounds painful now, but future you will be grateful in April, when taxes are due. You can use a tool like QuickBooks Self-Employed or just create a simple "Tax Fund" savings folder in your banking app.

If you regularly send invoices, create a simple template that lists the date, service, and amount due. Keep them in a single folder so you can track who has paid and who has not. Even a free Google Docs template works fine. You do not need fancy software to stay organized, just consistency.

When you are juggling multiple jobs or payments, prioritize essentials first. Picture your spending like a pyramid. Rent and food are the base, transportation and health come next, and extras like streaming or takeout sit at the top. If one of your gigs slows down or a client pays late, focus on the base until money evens out again.

A bare-minimum budget can help you survive slow months without panic. Write down only the basics you absolutely need, like rent, groceries, phone, and transportation. Keep that number somewhere visible. It is your emergency plan when things get tight. If income drops, you will already know exactly how much you need to stay afloat.

Unexpected Financial Hiccups

Unexpected expenses are part of gig life. Maybe your car breaks down or your laptop quits the day before a deadline. Having even a small buffer fund, $25 here or $40 there, can save you from overdraft fees or high-interest credit cards. Every time you earn more than expected, move a slice of that money into a buffer account. I call mine the "Oh Crap Fund." It is not fancy, but it works.

If you want to make it more fun, rename that fund in your banking app. Call it "Rainy Day," "Emergency Tacos," or "Future Me's Lifesaver." A little humor makes saving less painful and keeps you motivated.

Here is my real-life experience. A few years back, my rent was due, but my paycheck was delayed by my employer's payroll system. Instead of panicking, I messaged my landlord: "Hi, just a quick heads-up that my payment is delayed but should clear Friday morning. Can I drop off the rent then?" They appreciated the communication, and it saved me a late fee. The key is to stay proactive instead of hoping problems disappear.

Communication is everything when money involves other people. Send reminders, talk early, and be honest if you are struggling one month. It is easier to work something out before than to repair trust later. I have seen roommates stay friends for years because they were upfront about money, and others stop talking completely because they were not. Be in the first group.

Budgeting with roommates and gig work is not always smooth, but with the right tools and teamwork, you can keep the peace, avoid money drama, and still have cash left for takeout when things go right. The goal is progress, not perfection. Keep your systems simple, communicate often, and remember that learning to manage shared expenses is just another part of becoming financially confident.

No-Spend Challenges and Micro-Habits for Quick Wins

Sometimes your budget needs a reset—not a punishment or a guilt trip, just a quick refresh. That is where the no-spend challenge comes in. Think of it as a game you play with your wallet. For a set period, maybe seven days, two weeks, or even a month, you pause all unnecessary spending. Rent, groceries, and bills still get paid, but the extras take a break. No late-night Amazon scrolls, no "just one coffee" stops, and definitely no impulse "treat yourself" moments that somehow end with a new wardrobe.

The point is to pay attention to how you spend your money. You start to see the difference between what you need and what you do out of habit or boredom. The rules are up to you. Maybe you allow one social event a week or keep your morning coffee because you know skipping it would make everyone around you miserable. Decide your limits before you start so you are not negotiating with yourself in the snack aisle at 10:00 p.m.

To track your progress, create a no-spend calendar. You can draw it out on paper, use your phone, or even decorate a whiteboard. Mark every successful day with an "X," sticker, or emoji. Watching your streak grow feels surprisingly satisfying. If you make it seven days, celebrate. Then try 14, then 30. By the end of a month, you might realize how much random stuff you were buying that did not make you happier.

If you slip up during the challenge, and you probably will, it is fine. One unplanned fast food night does not ruin your progress. What matters is that you notice it and move on. Say, "Okay, that was off-plan, but I am back at it tomorrow." Perfection is not the goal; awareness is.

One of my friends did a 30-day no-spend challenge and lasted 18 days before caving on concert tickets. She felt guilty at first until she realized she had already saved more than $100 by cutting back elsewhere. She finished the rest of the challenge strong and told me later that it changed how she viewed spending for good.

Ideas for Money-Saving Micro-Habits

While no-spend challenges give you a reset, micro-habits help you build better money routines for the long haul. These are small, low-effort actions that make managing money automatic. You can start any of them today.

Try checking your bank balance once a day, maybe right after brushing your teeth or before checking social media. It takes less than a minute but keeps you aware of what is happening in your account.

You are less likely to overspend when you know your balance off the top of your head.

Another simple trick: Turn on transaction alerts in your banking app. Every time money leaves your account, you get a notification. It feels a little like your phone tattling on you ("Did you really need that delivery order?"), but it works.

Rounding up savings is another micro-habit worth using. Many banks and apps automatically round up your purchases to the nearest dollar and stash the extra change into savings. Buy something for $7.60, and 40 cents quietly moves into your savings account. It is sneaky progress, and it adds up faster than you think.

If you get paid in cash, drop your loose change or small bills into a jar each night. Label it with something that makes you smile: "Emergency Pizza," "Summer Adventure," or "Rainy-Day Backup." Watching it fill up is a visual reminder that small, consistent actions matter.

Micro-habits are not only about saving. They are also about awareness. You might create a rule that every time you buy something over $25, you pause for 24 hours first. This cooling-off period stops impulse buys and makes sure you actually want what you are about to purchase. Half the time, you will forget about the item completely, and your future self will thank you.

To make habits stick, make them visible. Use a simple habit tracker—draw a grid on paper or use an app. List your small money habits (like checking your balance, skipping takeout, or moving change into savings) and mark off each day you complete them. Over time, the satisfaction of keeping a streak going becomes addictive in the best way.

Quick-Start Habit Tracker

Draw a simple table with days of the week along the top and habits down the side:

Habit	Sun	Mon	Tue	Wed	Thu	Fri	Sat
No-Spend Day							
Checked Balance							
Saved Spare Change							

Color in each box or check it off as you complete the habit. Reward yourself at the end of the week with something simple and affordable, like watching a favorite movie, baking something from scratch, or a chill night with friends. Celebrate progress whenever you can.

Even with small wins, there will be slip-ups. Maybe you have a bad day and order delivery even though you swore you would cook. Or you buy something random online because it was "on sale." It happens. The trick is to treat it like a speed bump, not a wall. One purchase does not erase your progress. Just reset and keep going.

Some people like to make this fun by competing with a friend. See who can go the longest without takeout or who saves the most spare change in a month. A little friendly rivalry keeps it interesting and gives you someone to laugh with about your close calls later.

If you want a quick financial confidence boost, combine the two systems. Start a one-week no-spend challenge and pair it with one new micro-habit, like checking your balance daily. When the week ends, extend it another week and add one more habit, such as rounding up purchases. Layering small habits like this builds real momentum without burnout.

The best part about no-spend challenges and micro-habits is that they make saving feel like a series of small wins instead of a long, boring grind. You are not trying to overhaul your entire financial life overnight. You are just tweaking your daily routines. Each tiny step gives you a sense of progress, and over time, those steps add up to something powerful.

I remember the first time I tried a no-spend week. I thought it would feel restrictive, but instead, I felt in control for the first time. I lasted a day before slipping up, but I got back on track right after and kept going. That small reset showed me how many of my purchases came from boredom, not need. By the end of the week, I realized that saying "no" a little more often actually felt good, and that one experiment helped me rethink my habits permanently.

So start small. Pick a short challenge, try one or two micro-habits, and let the results motivate you. Whether you save $20 or S200, you will walk away with a better understanding of your money and a sense of pride that you are making progress, one smart decision at a time.

Remember that budgeting teaches you how to spend with purpose. Every dollar you track or habit you build gives you more control over how your money works for you. Up next, we'll talk about how to stretch every dollar further, spot sneaky spending traps, and still enjoy life without feeling like you're living on ramen and regret.

Budget Scenarios Challenge

Okay, you've learned the basics. Now, let's see how you'd handle real-life money situations. This section includes challenges based on what young adults actually go through.

Each scenario uses one of the budgeting methods you just learned: 50/30/20, Zero-Based, or Pay-Yourself-First. Your mission, should you choose to accept it, is to build a three-month budget for it. Don't stress about getting it perfect. There's no single "right" answer here. The goal is to practice, experiment, and see how each method fits different situations.

You'll find blank templates in the bonus section to help you map things out. When you're done, check out the sample solutions (also in the bonus section) to compare approaches and pick up a few new ideas for managing your own money.

Scenario 1: Josh and the Family Vacation (50/30/20 Budget)

Josh just landed a new job earning $2,400 a month after taxes. He rents a small apartment with a friend and wants to balance fun with responsibility. The first month with the new job goes smoothly, with no surprise bills or unexpected costs. Life is good.

As the calendar turns to the next month, Josh's parents announce a long weekend family vacation. They tell him it will cost about $600 for his share. Josh knows he can't really skip out because it is family, after all, and he has two months to save up. Since the trip falls on a holiday weekend, getting an extra day off from work should not be a problem. Now, he just needs a plan to make it all work.

Josh's fixed monthly expenses (including debt payments):

- Rent and utilities: $850
- Groceries: $200
- Phone: $100
- Transportation: $50
- Student loan: $280

Using the 50/30/20 Budgeting Method, build a three-month plan so Josh can pay for the trip without stress and still enjoy himself when he gets there.

Scenario 2: Samantha's Pay Raise (Pay-Yourself-First)

Samantha shares an apartment with two friends. Her job pays $1,800 a month after taxes, and while she doesn't have a car, she contributes to gas since one of her roommates drives. She's careful with her money and has clear goals: buying a car and saving for retirement. With that in mind, she's built a budget that comfortably covers her current expenses.

The following month, Samantha receives a promotion at work, increasing her take-home pay to $2,400 a month.

Samantha's fixed monthly expenses (including debt payments):

- Rent and utilities: $800
- Groceries: $250
- Phone: $40
- Transportation: $25
- Debt repayment: $100

60

Using the Pay-Yourself-First Budgeting Method, create a three-month plan for Samantha that helps her stay disciplined while putting her raise to work toward her goals.

Scenario 3: Alex's Job Loss (Zero-Based Budget)

Alex shares an apartment with his cousin. His income varies month to month depending on how many students need his tutoring services. His part-time job provides steady hours, but he still worries that his overall income isn't consistent or nearly enough. This month, Alex brings in $1,600 after taxes, a mix of his tutoring and part-time work. Fortunately, he's added a couple of new students for next month, boosting his expected income to $1,800.

Alex enjoys getting out, trying new things, and spending time with friends, but his unpredictable income makes that tough.

By month three, Alex faces one of life's toughest lessons: He loses his part-time job due to company cutbacks. For now, he'll have to rely solely on his tutoring income to make ends meet.

Alex's fixed monthly expenses (including debt payments):

- Rent and utilities: $650
- Groceries: $200
- Phone: $90
- Transportation: $60
- Debt repayment: $125

Using the Zero-Based Budgeting Method, design a three-month plan that captures Alex's changing income and shows how he can stay on track even when life throws him a curveball.

Chapter 4

Smart Spending
Making Your Money Go Further

Tracking Your Spending: From Tap-to-Pay to Venmo

Ever open your banking app at month's end and wonder if your money packed its bags and left without saying goodbye? Yeah, me too. Between grabbing snacks with a quick tap, sending your friends pizza money, and covering rideshares and lattes with barely a thought, it's easy to lose track of what's leaving your account. Digital payments make spending feel effortless, almost invisible. That's great for convenience but not so great for staying in control of your money.

These days, cash rarely leaves our hands, so we lose that "ouch" moment of handing over bills. When money moves with a quick tap, it's like it never existed. The result? Tiny, sneaky leaks in your budget that add up fast. Tracking your spending helps you spot those leaks before they flood your financial boat.

Start by getting all your transactions in one place. Most bank apps show every debit, credit, or tap-to-pay purchase, so scroll through your recent history and see what's really going on. Take 10 minutes to review the past month's charges. You might spot patterns you didn't notice before, like $60 on delivery fees or three "forgotten" subscriptions.

Venmo or Cash App lets you download statements. In Venmo, tap "Statements" under Settings. In Cash App, tap "Export CSV." You'll get a spreadsheet with every payment, who it went to, and what it was for. Pop that file into Google Sheets or Excel and see where your money is actually going.

Many modern banking apps, like Chime, Ally, or Capital One, automatically sort transactions into categories such as Food, Entertainment, and Transportation. You'll often see a colorful pie chart that visually shows where your spending lands. Spoiler: Food and Dining is usually bigger than we expect.

If you're old school or just prefer writing things down, a spending journal or simple spreadsheet still works. Sometimes the act of writing "$8 coffee" next to "Tuesday morning" is enough to make you rethink doing it three times a week.

Automated apps like PocketGuard and YNAB (You Need A Budget) take it further. PocketGuard calculates what's safe to spend after bills and savings goals, while YNAB helps you assign every dollar a purpose, whether that's groceries, bills, or fun money. Both let you connect your bank accounts and track everything in real time.

If you prefer a light touch, most banks now let you set up daily or weekly balance alerts. You'll get a quick ping if your spending starts running wild, giving you a chance to rein it back in before it turns into a problem.

Interactive Element: Monthly Spending Audit Worksheet

Spend 10 minutes on this mini–financial reality check:

1. Export your bank and Venmo or Cash App transactions for the past 30 days.
2. Sort them into simple categories such as Food, Transportation, Subscriptions, Shopping, and Fun money.
3. Add up each category. No rounding down. Be honest.

4. Highlight the areas that surprised you (looking at you, "food delivery").
5. Jot down one change you'll make next month.

When I did this for the first time, I realized my "quick lunches" at work added up to over $160 in a month. That hit harder than my gym fee, and I didn't even get abs out of it.

The point of this exercise isn't guilt; it's clarity. Seeing where your money goes gives you power. You can't change what you don't track.

Digital payments make it easy to lose awareness of where our money flows, but with just a little attention, you can turn that around. Start small. Maybe you only track your food spending this month or set one alert for your checking balance. You'll build momentum without feeling overwhelmed.

Smart spending involves knowing where your money goes so you can decide what's worth it and what's just noise. A few minutes of awareness each week can save you from that end-of-month panic when your balance looks suspiciously lower than you remember.

Mastering the "Bougie on a Budget" Flex

Being "bougie on a budget" means living well without draining your account. To do so, you need to be clever. You can still enjoy life's luxuries without paying full price. The secret is to get creative, plan ahead, and make small swaps that feel like upgrades instead of sacrifices.

Take coffee, for example. I once realized I was spending more on cold brew than my internet bill. Now I make café-level drinks at home using a $15 milk frother and a dash of cinnamon. The flavor is great, the foam looks fancy, and the savings add up fast. That's $30–40 a week back in my pocket, money that now funds my "treat yourself" dinners instead of overpriced caffeine.

Clothing is another goldmine for smart spending. Thrift and resale shops like Depop and Poshmark are full of hidden gems. "Vintage" Levi's for $12? Yes, please. Want the designer look without the price tag? Search online for "dupes," which are high-quality alternatives that look nearly identical to the real thing. Just check reviews and return policies before you start thinking you discovered fashion's best-kept secret.

Your living space can get the same glow-up. Try peel-and-stick wallpaper, new lampshades from thrift stores, or LED light strips. Throw pillows and discount candles go a long way toward making a room feel like a boutique hotel without needing a trust fund.

Self-care doesn't have to cost spa prices, either. A DIY face mask, Epsom salt bath, and a chill playlist can rival a professional treatment. Personally, I'm more of a "long shower, good playlist, and lights dimmed" kind of person. Same relaxation, zero booking fee.

Timing also matters. Big retailers have predictable sale cycles: January for linens, February for electronics, and August for laptops. Combine that with browser extensions like Honey or Rakuten, and you'll catch discounts that make you feel like you just hacked capitalism.

"Bougie on a budget" works because it's personal. Decide which small luxuries make you happiest and spend there while trimming back in other spots. Love candles? Go for it. Prefer staying in to eating out? Perfect, splurge on quality ingredients and host a "fake restaurant" night at home. The goal is balance, not restriction.

Worksheet: Where Do I Want to Treat Myself?

Answer these questions in your notes app or journal:

- What makes me feel "upgraded" or confident?
- Where does my FOMO hit hardest?
- Which splurges were worth it and which flopped?
- What can I skip to fund what actually matters?

When I did this exercise, I realized clothes didn't excite me, but good food did. Once I started cooking more at home, I could afford occasional nice dinners guilt-free. Find your version of that.

Smart spending means you are outspending your budget without depriving yourself. When someone compliments your outfit or your setup, it's extra satisfying to say, "Thanks, got it on sale, and no, I'm not telling you where."

Subscription Overload: Cancel Culture for Your Wallet

Subscriptions have a sneaky way of multiplying. You start with one free trial, and suddenly your bank statement looks like a shopping list of forgotten charges. Spotify, Netflix, Adobe, Disney+, Xbox, and that random meditation app you used once all quietly nibble away at your wallet. Each one feels harmless, but together they can drain hundreds of dollars a year.

The fix starts with a subscription audit. Open your email and search for words like "receipt," "renewal," or "subscription." Then check your bank or PayPal history for repeat charges over the past 60 days. You will probably find at least one you forgot existed. I found two, and one was for a photo-editing app that sounded good at the time.

If that sounds like a hassle, use an app like Rocket Money. It scans your accounts for subscriptions, flags upcoming renewals, and can even cancel some automatically.

Once you have your list, go line by line and ask yourself:

- *Do I still use this regularly?*
- *Would I miss it if it were gone?*
- *Is there a cheaper or free alternative?*

If you answer yes, keep it. If you hesitate, pause or rotate it for a month. And if the answer is no, cancel it and enjoy that satisfying little victory dance when your next statement comes in lower.

To figure out what is truly worth keeping, calculate your cost per use. Take the monthly fee and divide it by how often you use the service. If you paid $15 for a streaming app and only watched three shows, that is $5 per use, which is not a great deal. Compare that to your favorite platform that costs $10, but you used it 10 times. That is one dollar per use and much easier to justify.

Subscription	Monthly Fee	Days Used	Cost per Use
Disney+	$10	3	$3.33
Netflix	$15	10	$1.50
Gym App	$15	0	N/A
Magazine App	$8	0	N/A

When it is time to cancel, skip the guilt trip. Some apps try to tug at your heartstrings with messages like *"Are you sure you want to leave us?"* You are not breaking up with anyone. You are just keeping your wallet healthy.

For tricky services that require a phone call or chat, keep it short and polite:

"Hi, I would like to cancel my subscription effective immediately. Please confirm there will be no further charges."

If they offer a special deal to stay, only take it if you genuinely plan to use it. Otherwise, smile, hang up, and move on.

Free trials deserve extra attention. Set a calendar reminder two days before each trial ends. Include the name of the service and your login details. That tiny bit of effort will save you from accidental renewals later.

If you miss something after canceling, you can always resubscribe later. Some people rotate streaming services. One month of Sling, one of Netflix, then Disney+. It keeps your options fresh and your spending low.

Splitting and Sharing

Sharing costs is one of the smartest moves you can make. If you live with roommates, friends, or family, split subscriptions fairly. Many services, such as Spotify, Apple Music, and Netflix, offer family plans that allow multiple users. Just check the fine print so you don't accidentally break the "same household" rule.

Use Venmo or another payment app to automate reminders for everyone's share. No one enjoys chasing payments, so set it and forget it. A quick "Hey, Spotify is due Friday, sending reminders now" message works wonders.

Keep What Brings You Value

At the end of the day, this is not about living subscription-free. It is about keeping what truly adds joy or convenience and ditching what does not. Maybe Apple Music is your daily motivation, but that meal-kit plan keeps turning into food waste. Let your real habits decide what is worth paying for.

Keep an updated list of active subscriptions in your notes app or Google Doc. Review it every few months, or whenever your finances feel tight. Subscriptions slip in quietly, and if you do not keep an eye on them, they multiply faster than free trials on YouTube Premium.

Each small cancellation feels good, like deleting junk emails for your bank account. The result is more breathing room, fewer random charges, and the relief of knowing exactly where your money goes.

How to Say No (Without Losing Friends or Fun)

Turning down expensive plans can feel awkward. Maybe your friends are planning a $40 brunch or a last-minute concert, and you are thinking, *I really shouldn't*, but also, *I don't want to be the boring one*. The truth? Everyone has been there. Saying no does not make you cheap; it makes you smart about your priorities.

Remember, saying no now is not saying no forever. It is just a pause. When I first started tracking my spending, I had to turn down a few hangouts. I worried I would miss out, but instead, I found cheaper ways to connect, like backyard dinners, game nights, or coffee walks that did not drain my checking account.

If you dread the moment when you have to explain, try having a few ready lines:

- *"I wish I could, but it is not in my budget this week. Rain check?"*
- *"I am on a spending freeze right now. Want to hang at my place instead?"*
- *"I am saving for something big, so I am sitting this one out."*

Text it, say it, or drop it casually in a group chat. No long explanation needed. You will be surprised by how many people respond with "Same!" or "Good idea." Most folks are relieved someone finally said what they were thinking.

Suggesting Alternatives

Offering cheaper ideas keeps the social vibe alive. Skip dinner out and host a potluck or picnic. If concert tickets are too pricey, stream a live show or make a themed playlist night. Sometimes, the fun is not in the spending; it is in being together.

I once suggested "cheap eats night" when my friends wanted to try an expensive restaurant. We each made a dish at home and met up to share. It cost less than ten bucks per person, and honestly, the food was better than the restaurant. Plus, we argued over whose pasta was best, so free entertainment was included.

Owning Your Money Goals

Being upfront about your goals will earn respect. It takes guts to say, "I am saving for a car," or "I am building my emergency fund." It shows you are focused, not frugal. The right friends will get it, and some might even join you.

Setting Boundaries

If your social circle keeps suggesting pricey plans, set expectations early. Post something like, "Trying to save this month. Down for game nights or coffee instead!" That quick note prevents awkward invites later and saves everyone a little guilt.

Fun Without the Splurge

Having fun does not require spending. Try:

- Board game or trivia nights with free apps
- Movie marathons with homemade popcorn
- Local hikes or park days
- Free community concerts or art walks

- Rotating "hangout at home" nights with friends

These kinds of nights often become the best memories because there is zero pressure to impress anyone. You can laugh louder, wear sweatpants, and still have the time of your life.

The Ultimate Guide to Scoring Deals, Discounts, and Student Perks

Few things feel better than seeing that little "promo code applied" message at checkout. Saving $20 might not change your life, but it sure feels like a win. That is the beauty of smart spending: You get the same stuff for less. With so many tools and apps available, saving money can become second nature.

Your first step is to make saving automatic. Browser extensions like Honey and Rakuten are must-haves. Honey searches for coupon codes at checkout and applies the best one. Rakuten gives you cash back when you shop through its link. Installation takes a couple of minutes, and the savings add up fast.

If you shop online often, use both. Honey finds instant discounts, and Rakuten pays you later. I once got a $42 Rakuten check in the mail. It felt like free money for things I was already going to buy.

If you are a student, your school email is a money-saving cheat code. Platforms like UNiDAYS and Student Beans verify your status and unlock discounts on Apple, Adidas, Grubhub, Spotify, and many more. You will often get 10–25% off without any extra effort. Some of the best deals include:

- **Spotify + Hulu Student Plan:** Often half-price, sometimes bundled
- **Apple Education Store:** Discounts on MacBooks, iPads, and accessories

- **Adobe Creative Cloud:** Big savings if you need Photoshop or Illustrator
- **Amazon Prime Student:** Six months free, then half off the regular rate
- **Microsoft Office:** Free with many school emails

I used my student email for Spotify and Hulu, and it felt like winning a lifetime subscription.

Once you start stacking discounts, it gets addictive in the best way. Suppose you are buying sneakers online: Find a 15% UNiDAYS discount, add a 10% Honey code, click through Rakuten for 5% cash back, and pay with a credit card that gives 2% back. That $100 pair is now much closer to $70. Saving money starts to feel like a sport.

Loyalty Programs and Shopping Secrets

Loyalty programs are another easy win. Grocery stores, gas stations, and retail shops all offer them, and rewards build faster than you expect. Target Circle gives 1% back plus birthday coupons. Sephora Beauty Insider sends you free samples. Starbucks Rewards turns caffeine into free drinks, and CVS ExtraCare sends instant coupons straight to your app. My rule: If I shop somewhere more than twice a year, I join the rewards program. It is free money, plain and simple.

Here is one more secret that works surprisingly well: just ask. Most people never ask for discounts because it feels awkward, but you would be amazed at how often it pays off. In person or online, try asking, *"Do you offer a student or first-time customer discount?"* or *"I saw another store has a promo; can you match it?"* A friend of mine shaved $10 off her phone bill by asking. Another got half off a gym membership after mentioning a competitor's price. I once saved $40 at a camera shop just by asking if the sample was cheaper. Sometimes the best hack is just confidence.

The magic happens when you combine all of this. Before you hit "Buy," take 30 seconds to check: Did I search for a coupon code? Can I use a cash back site? Do I qualify for a loyalty or student discount? Can I pay with a rewards card? Once this becomes a reflex, you will rarely pay full price again.

Keep a quick "Savings Stack" note in your phone. Add your favorite tools such as Honey, Rakuten, UNiDAYS, Target Circle, Sephora Insider, and Starbucks Rewards. Jot down the best sale months: January for linens, February for electronics, May for furniture, August for back to school, and November for tech. Planning your purchases beats impulse every single time.

A few months ago, I wanted noise-canceling headphones that retailed for $180. I waited for a seasonal sale, used a 10% UNiDAYS discount, got another 5% through Rakuten, and paid with a 2% cash back card. Total cost: $118. The $62 I did not spend went straight into savings. Little wins like that build real progress.

If you are making a big purchase, such as a laptop or gym membership, ask if there is a promo or student rate. Many reps have unadvertised discounts they can apply. Timing matters, too. Want a laptop? Wait for back to school or Black Friday. Need sneakers? Try early spring, when new models arrive and last season's shoes get marked down.

The trick is not just buying less. It is buying smarter. Use the tools, stack the deals, and be intentional about where your money goes. A bargain that sits unused is not a bargain. The satisfaction of scoring a deal that fits your budget and your lifestyle never gets old. And if anyone calls you cheap, remind them you are not cutting corners; you are cutting costs.

You've officially leveled up your spending game. At this point, you can sniff out a discount faster than a dog finds dropped pizza crust. You've learned how to stretch your cash, shop smart, and keep more of your paycheck where it belongs, right in your account.

Now that you've got the saving side down, it's time to tackle the next big piece of the puzzle: credit. Don't worry: This isn't the scary credit-card-debt horror story chapter. We're talking about using credit as a tool, not a trap. In Chapter 5, you'll learn how credit scores work, what really matters, and how to build a financial foundation that opens doors instead of slamming them shut.

Chapter 5

Credit Confidence

Building and Protecting
Your Credit the Right Way

Credit Scores Decoded: What Actually Matters

You can be cruising through life, filling out an apartment application or trying to finance your first car, when suddenly you get denied because of a "credit score." This mysterious three-digit number quietly determines whether you get approved for big milestones like renting, buying a car, setting up utilities, or even getting a new phone plan. It's basically a financial report card that follows you everywhere.

Life Milestones That Credit Impacts

- Renting an apartment (landlords almost always check)
- Getting approved for a car loan or lease
- Qualifying for a credit card or student card
- Setting up utilities without a big deposit
- Getting a postpaid phone plan
- Some companies run credit checks on potential employees

Your credit score shows lenders how trustworthy you are with borrowed money. The most common type, the FICO score, ranges from 300 to 850. Higher is better. A solid score opens doors years down the road, while a poor one can shut them, at least temporarily.

So what matters in a credit score? Let's break down the five big factors behind your score.

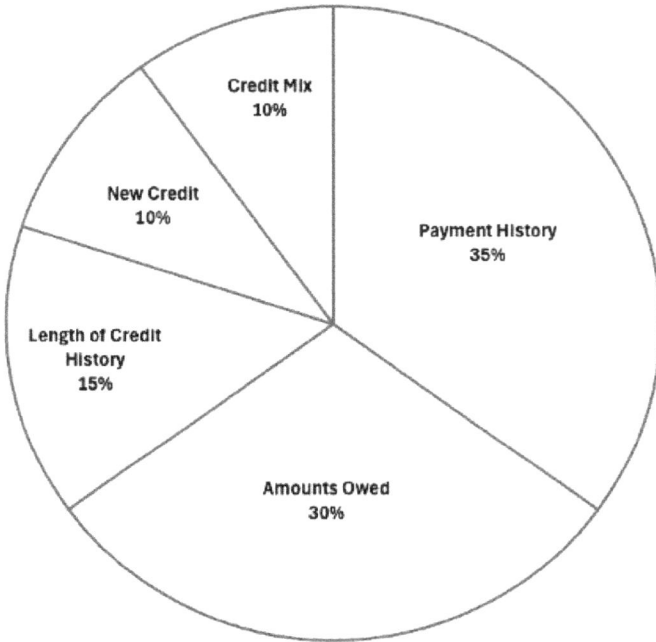

Credit Mix
10%

New Credit
10%

Payment History
35%

Length of Credit History
15%

Amounts Owed
30%

- **Payment history (35%):** Pay on time. Even the minimum. One late payment can hurt your score for years, so hit those due dates.
- **Accounts owed (30%):** Keep your balance low compared to your limit. If you have a $1,000 limit, stay under $300. Less is always better.
- **Length of credit history (15%):** The longer your accounts are open, the better. Old cards are your friends.
- **New credit inquiries (10%):** Each time you apply for a new card, your score dips a little.
- **Credit mix (10%):** Lenders like variety, such as cards and loans, but this isn't critical early on.

Myth-Busting Quick Guide

Now, let's bust a few myths before they sneak up on you.

- **Checking your own credit score?** Totally safe. That's a soft inquiry, and it doesn't hurt you.
- **Debit cards?** They don't build credit. They're great for managing cash, but they don't count toward your score.
- **Your income, age, or job title?** Irrelevant. A barista and a brain surgeon start on equal ground.
- **Paying off collections?** This helps, but the mark sticks around for a while.
- **Closing old cards?** This can lower your score by reducing your average account age.

When lenders report your account info to Experian, Equifax, and TransUnion, your score shifts monthly based on your balances, payments, and activity.

Miss a payment? Don't panic. If you're a few days late, you'll probably just pay a late fee (ouch). But once you hit 30 days, the credit bureaus find out, and your score can drop anywhere from 60 to 100 points. Thankfully, that damage fades with time, just like your old middle-school haircut.

The secret to great credit is consistency. Pay on time, keep your balances low, and stop stressing about perfection. Credit grows quietly when you're consistent.

Safe Ways to Start Building Credit (Even if You're Nervous)

Building credit for the first time can feel a little scary. You've heard horror stories about debt spirals, late payments, and people tanking their score before they even know what "credit utilization" means. The good news? You can start slow, safe, and smart. No risk-taking required.

Option 1: The Secured Credit Card

Think of this as credit with training wheels. You make a small cash deposit, usually between $200 and $500, and that becomes your credit limit. If you forget to pay, the bank simply uses your deposit. It's a great way to prove you're responsible without the risk of going into debt.

Use it for small things like gas or streaming services, then pay the balance in full each month. Within a few months, you'll start seeing progress on your credit score. When I first started, I used mine for one purchase a month just to stay organized. It worked.

Option 2: The Student Credit Card

If you're a student, you're in luck. Student cards are made for beginners. They come with low limits, easy approval, and sometimes small perks for good grades or on-time payments. Finally, a reward system that actually benefits you for being responsible.

Option 3: Authorized User Status

If your parents or another trusted adult has good credit, ask to be added as an authorized user. You'll benefit from their positive payment history, which can help boost your score faster. Make sure to agree on boundaries and communication ahead of time. This isn't a free shopping spree card; it's a shared responsibility. I like to call it a "credit curfew." You both know what's okay to spend, and everyone sleeps better at night.

Comparison Table: Starter Credit Options

Method	Pros	Cons
Secured Credit Card	Low risk, east approval	Requires deposit, small limit
Student Credit Card	Student perks, no deposit, rewards	May need income or co-signer
Authorized User	Leverage's another's good history	Affected if primary user misses payment

Before you apply for anything, do a little homework. Look for cards with no annual fee, a clear mobile app, and an automatic payment option. Apps that send alerts for spending and due dates are life-savers. Some banks even let you set up "safe to spend" notifications that remind you if your balance starts getting close to your limit. That little ping can save you from an accidental overcharge or a late-night impulse buy.

Once you're approved, set up automatic payments immediately. Even paying the minimum amount on time helps your score. If you can pay your balance in full every month, even better, because you'll avoid interest altogether. I once forgot to set up autopay on a new card and got hit with a $29 late fee for being two days late. Never again. Automation is the closest thing to a financial cheat code.

Here's a quick rule of thumb: Use less than 30% of your available limit. If your limit is $300, keep your balance under $90. This ratio, called credit utilization, is one of the fastest ways to strengthen your score. If you can, aim even lower, around 10%, to really impress lenders. Paying off your balance early in the month, before the state-ment closes, can also boost your score faster since it shows a smaller balance being reported.

Having just one card and using it wisely is plenty to get started. You don't need multiple accounts. Good credit is built by consistency, not quantity. Think of it like working out: Doing a few reps regularly beats overdoing it once and quitting. Focus on forming the habit first, then build from there.

If you're wondering which cards to start with, these are all solid picks:

Card	Best Features	Potential Drawbacks	Ideal For
Discover it Student Card	Cash-back rewards, no annual fee, free FICO score	Approval not guaranteed; must show income or student status	Students starting to build credit
Capital One Journey Student	No annual fee, credit limit can grow with on-time payments	May require some credit or income history	First-time cardholders building reliability
Chime Credit Builder	No hard credit check, no annual fee, helps build history safely	Must have Chime account & direct deposits; no rewards	Beginners wanting a low-risk card

Once you're comfortable, you can explore other cards with rewards that match your lifestyle, like travel points or cash back on groceries. But don't rush it. Credit is like reputation: It builds slowly through reliability and good behavior.

You can think of building credit like learning to ride a bike. You wobble a bit at first, but once you get the rhythm of paying on time and staying organized, it becomes second nature. And unlike riding a bike, you won't need a helmet, just a few good habits and some patience. Before long, you'll look back and realize your credit is cruising along smoothly, and you didn't crash once.

Credit Cards 101: Choosing, Using, and Avoiding Debt Traps

Credit cards are great tools when handled right, but they can turn on you fast if you don't understand how they work. Don't think of a credit card as free money; it's borrowed money with a deadline and a bill waiting to be paid.

Your goal isn't to fear credit, but to use it smartly. That's how people with good credit scores look calm at the checkout line. They've learned the secret: Use your card for convenience, not for cash you don't have.

Checklist: What to Look for in Your First Card

- $0 annual fee
- Low APR (preferably under 25%; always try to pay in full anyway)
- Grace period of at least 21 days
- Straightforward rewards (cash back or usable points)
- Useful app with real-time updates
- Responsive customer service (check online reviews)

Key Terms Table

At a minimum, you need to know these terms when you have a credit card:

Term	What it Means
APR	Annual Percentage Rate - the interest charged if you don't pay in full
Annual Fee	Yearly fee to keep the card - avoid unless perks clearly outweigh the cost
Grace Period	Days between statement and due date - pay during this to skip interest
Minimum Payment	Smallest acceptable payment - only paying this racks up debt fast

When comparing cards, don't get dazzled by fancy rewards or airline miles that you'll never use. Most beginners do best with a simple cash-back card. Even one percent back adds up over time. Plus, it keeps your focus where it matters: paying on time and keeping balances low.

Before applying, look closely at the fine print. Watch for things like "intro APRs," "balance transfer fees," and sneaky annual charges that kick in after the first year. A credit card should work for you, not trap you in unnecessary costs.

Use It Like a Debit Card With Benefits

Here's the golden rule: Treat your credit card like a debit card with perks. Only buy what you can afford to pay off when the bill arrives. Using it for one or two predictable expenses, such as gas, groceries, or a streaming subscription, makes things easy to track. This keeps your usage consistent and builds good habits without overwhelming you.

Once you have your first card, set up automatic payments right away. Even if you can only pay the minimum some months, making payments on time is what matters most. Ideally, pay the full balance each month so you never pay interest. That's where true financial power comes from: spending smart, paying responsibly, and never giving the bank a reason to charge you more.

If you ever slip, don't panic. Mistakes happen. Call your bank and say, "Hi, I noticed I missed a payment. This is my first time. Can you waive the fee?" You'd be surprised how often they'll do it. Politeness pays—in this case, literally.

The Danger Zone: Common Credit Card Traps

Credit card companies love offering "no interest for six months" deals. Sounds amazing, right? But here's the catch: If you don't pay off the full balance by the end of that promo period, they'll retroactively charge you all the interest you thought you avoided. That "no interest" furniture or laptop can end up costing more than retail if you miss the deadline by even one day. Unless you've set aside the money and are absolutely sure you can pay it off in time, skip these offers.

Also, avoid cash advances whenever possible. Banks start charging interest immediately, often at higher rates, and sometimes with an extra five percent fee on top. Borrowing $100 could cost you $110 within weeks. It's rarely worth it.

Minimum payments might look harmless, but they're sneaky. If you owe $500 and only pay the $25 minimum, it could take you nearly two years to pay it off, and you'll hand over another $100 or more in interest along the way. Always pay more than the minimum, even if it's just a few extra dollars. Every little bit chips away at the balance faster.

Real-Life Example: My Friend Who Learned the Hard Way

My friend Taylor got their first credit card in college. They used it for "small things," like coffee, gas, and concert tickets. It didn't feel like much until the first bill came in at $600. They paid the minimum, shrugged, and kept spending. A few months later, they owed over $900. One day, Taylor finally looked at the statement closely and realized almost $200 of that total was just interest. They stopped using the card for a while, started paying double the minimum, and eventually paid it off. Lesson learned. The next card they got, they set it to autopay and used it only for their phone bill. Their credit score climbed 120 points in a year.

The takeaway is simple: The system rewards responsibility, not avoidance. If you manage credit with intention, it works for you. If you ignore it, it works against you.

Requesting a Higher Limit (The Right Way)

Once you've built a few months of positive history, you can request a higher credit limit. Think of it like leveling up in a game. You've proven you can handle the starter level, so now you unlock "Credit Limit Plus." A higher limit helps your score because it lowers your utilization ratio, even if you spend the same amount.

But here's the catch: A higher limit isn't permission to start impulse shopping. It's not the universe telling you to go wild on takeout or late-night online deals. It's more like your bank saying, "We trust you not to do anything questionable." Keep that trust. Use the higher limit to strengthen your credit score, not to fund random purchases.

Call your bank or use the app to request an increase. Most issuers will review your account and, if you've paid on time and avoided carrying big balances, they'll usually say yes. Sometimes they'll do a "soft pull" on your credit, which doesn't affect your score, just to make sure everything looks good.

Use that new breathing room wisely. Keep your spending habits the same, enjoy the quiet score boost, and give yourself a little mental high-five for adulting responsibly. And if you treat yourself to a coffee to celebrate, make sure you pay it off before the due date. You've earned it.

How to Check Your Credit for Free (And What to Do If It's Low)

Checking your credit doesn't have to feel like a horror movie where you peek through your fingers, hoping it's not that bad. It's easy, free, and way less scary than you think.

Start at AnnualCreditReport.com, the only website approved by federal law to give you free reports from all three major bureaus: Experian, Equifax, and TransUnion. You get one free report from each company every year, so a smart move is to space them out by checking one every four months. That way, you're keeping tabs year-round without paying a dime.

If you want to check more often, use Credit Karma or the Experian app. Both are free, legitimate, and helpful. They won't show your exact FICO score, but they'll give you a solid idea of where you stand and what's helping or hurting your credit.

Once you've got your report, start by checking that your personal information is correct. Make sure your name, address, and accounts all look familiar. If you see something off, such as a mysterious

"Nebraska address" when you've never been west of Ohio, that's a red flag.

Then, review your accounts. Every credit card, loan, and payment history should look accurate. Highlight anything unusual, like accounts you never opened or payments marked late that you know were on time.

If you spot an error, don't panic. Each bureau has an online dispute form where you can explain the issue and upload proof such as bank statements or screenshots. It's free, and they are legally required to investigate within 30 days. If they confirm the mistake, your report updates automatically. Your score usually improves within a month or two.

Now, if your score looks lower than you hoped, take a breath. It's fixable. Here's your five-step recovery plan:

1. **Pay every bill on time.** Payment history is king. Even one late payment can hurt, so set reminders or automate your bills.
2. **Lower your balances.** Try to use less than 30% of your credit limit. If you can, aim for 10% or less. It shows lenders you're not stretching too thin.
3. **Don't close your oldest card.** That card might look dusty, but it's helping your credit age, which boosts your score.
4. **Add positive accounts.** A secured or student credit card can jumpstart your progress if you're rebuilding.
5. **Check your score regularly.** Make it a habit to track your progress every few months and stay in control.

One reader told me she dropped 80 points after missing a payment during finals week. She set up autopay, paid off her balance, and within six months her score bounced back even higher than before. That's the beauty of credit: It rewards consistency, not perfection.

So, if your score isn't where you want it yet, don't treat it like a permanent grade. Think of it as a report that updates every month. Keep doing the right things, and the numbers will catch up. Your future self will thank you when that "Approved!" message finally pops up.

Swipe Left on Debt: Overcoming Credit Card Anxiety and Mistakes

Debt happens to good people all the time. You buy textbooks, groceries, or concert tickets thinking you'll pay them off next month, and then interest sneaks in like a raccoon at two in the morning. Suddenly that "temporary" balance turns into a full-time roommate you didn't invite.

If you only make minimum payments, you'll end up paying far more than the item ever cost. For instance, if you charge $800 at 22% APR and only pay $30 a month. It will take you almost three years to pay it off, and you'll end up paying over $250 in interest.

Mistakes happen, so skip the guilt spiral. Everyone slips up at some point. The key is to take action fast. Pay what you can right away, even if it's just the minimum, and then call your credit card company. Explain what happened and ask for help. Many lenders offer hardship programs, temporary lower rates, or will even waive late fees if you've been responsible before. It's much easier to fix a stumble early than to dig out months later.

Strategies for Paying off Debt

If your debt feels like it's growing faster than you can handle, pick a strategy and stick with it. The two most popular methods are:

1. **Snowball Method:** Focus on paying off your smallest balance first. The quick win gives you momentum and motivation. Once that first card is gone, move to the next smallest.
2. **Avalanche Method:** Start with the balance that has the highest interest rate. It saves you more money overall, though progress may feel slower at first.

There's no wrong choice. The best method is the one that keeps you motivated and consistent. I prefer the snowball method because watching one balance hit zero feels amazing. It's a small victory that keeps you going.

You can also automate your payments. Set up automatic transfers for at least the minimum amount, then make extra payments whenever you have a good week or a side gig payout. Even $20 here and there helps because it chips away at future interest.

If you ever feel like your debt is controlling you instead of the other way around, you're not alone. Free help exists, and it's good help. The National Foundation for Credit Counseling (NFCC) offers confidential guidance, helps you build repayment plans, and can even negotiate with creditors to lower interest rates. If you're in school, your financial aid office might also have staff who specialize in financial coaching. Don't be afraid to ask. It's literally their job to help you get back on track.

A friend once told me, "Three late payments tanked my score sophomore year. I thought I was doomed, but I rebuilt it one on-time payment at a time." Two years later, his score was back in the high

700s, and he was approved for his first car loan. Proof that credit recovery is about progress, not perfection.

When you understand how debt works, it loses its power to intimidate you. You've now learned how to manage credit, recover from setbacks, and rebuild confidence one choice at a time. Up next comes one of the biggest financial hurdles young adults face: student loans. They might look intimidating, but with the right plan, they're completely manageable and won't derail your future.

Chapter 6

Student Loan Survival

From FAFSA to Fast Payoff

Student Loans Demystified: Federal vs. Private, Subsidized vs. Unsubsidized

When that financial-aid email lands, all the numbers and terms can feel like alphabet soup. I remember opening mine and thinking, *Is this a loan or a math test?* Understanding the basics now can save you thousands later.

The two main types of loans are federal and private.

- **Federal loans** are backed by the government. They come with fixed interest rates, flexible repayment plans, income-based options, and sometimes forgiveness for public-service careers. You access them through the FAFSA (Free Application for Federal Student Aid), and they should almost always be your first choice.
- **Private loans** come from banks, credit unions, or online lenders. Approval depends on creditworthiness (often with a co-signer), and rates can change. They rarely include safety nets such as income-driven repayment or forgiveness, so treat them as a last resort.

Here's a quick summary:

Feature	Federal Loans	Private Loans
Source	U.S. Government	Banks/lenders
Interest Rate	Fixed, usually low	Variable or fixed
Credit Check Needed	Not for most	Yes
Repayment Flexibility	High	Limited
Deferment/Forbearance	Yes	Varies
Forgiveness Options	Yes (some jobs)	Rare
Subsidized Option	Yes (if qualified)	No

If you borrow both types, remember that federal loans let you adjust payments when income drops. Private lenders expect full payment regardless of your situation.

Within federal loans, you'll see two flavors: subsidized and unsubsidized.

- **Subsidized loans** are need-based, and the government covers your interest while you're in school at least half-time.
- **Unsubsidized loans** start accruing interest the moment they're disbursed.

Let's say two students borrow $3,500 each year. The subsidized borrower owes exactly $14,000 after four years. The unsubsidized borrower, at 5% interest, owes roughly $15,840. That extra $1,840 is interest quietly piling up.

Each year, review your financial-aid award letter carefully. Look for labels such as "Federal Direct Subsidized Loan" or "Unsubsidized Loan." If anything looks unclear, call the financial-aid office. They like it when students ask smart questions.

A sample award letter might look like this:

2026-2027 Financial Aid Offer

Dear [Student Name],

We are pleased to share your financial aid package for the academic year 2026-2027. Please review the details below. If you have questions or notice any discrepancies, contact the Financial Aid Office. We are here to help.

Grants and Scholarships (do not need to be repaid):

Federal Pell Grant	$3,200

Loans (must be repaid):

Federal Direct Subsidized Loan	$3,500
Federal Direct Unsubsidized Loan	$2,000
Parent PLUS Loan (optional)	$4,000
Private/Alternative Loan (optional; application required)	$X

Work-Study (part-time job opportunity):

Work-Study	$1,500

Please read the terms carefully, especially for loans, and accept or decline the aid through your student portal.

Sincerely,

Financial Aid Office

Before accepting loans, pause and ask:

- Do I really need the full amount?
- Is this loan subsidized or unsubsidized?

- Have I used all federal options before considering private ones?
- When does interest start accruing?

Borrow only what you need. You can always reduce an accepted loan before disbursement.

Checklist: Know Before You Borrow

- List every loan type from your aid letter.
- Confirm which are subsidized.
- Note each interest rate and start date.
- Verify that amounts are confirmed, not estimated.
- Accept only what you truly need.
- Contact your financial aid office with any questions.

Never sign until everything makes sense. Future you will appreciate that 10-minute double-check.

Repayment Options Explained–Choosing Your Best Path After Graduation

Graduation feels amazing until that first student loan bill shows up. One minute you're tossing your cap in the air, and the next, you're opening an email that says "Payment Due." It's a quick dose of adult reality. But the good news? Federal loans come with options, flexibility, and a bit of breathing room if you know where to look.

Federal loans offer several repayment plans designed for different life stages and income levels. Think of them as paths up the same mountain: one is steep but quick, another is longer with scenic stops along the way, and one even lets you pause for a snack when your budget gets tight.

You can explore all of these using the Loan Simulator at StudentAid.gov. Enter your loan total, estimated income, and family size, and it will show you side-by-side comparisons. For example, a $30,000 federal loan might cost $322 per month under the Standard Plan, but only about $110 with an income-driven (IDR) plan. The tradeoff is time; you will pay longer and more in total interest, but you will stay afloat while your income grows.

A lot of borrowers start with an IDR plan and switch later once their salary increases. It is not permanent. You can change your plan at any time, and that flexibility can save you from falling behind during low-income stretches.

Here's a quick comparison:

Plan	Monthly Payment	Term Length	Best for
Standard	Fixed, higher	10 years	Stable income, want fast payoff
Graduated	Starts low, rises	10 years	Expecting raises
Extended	Lower, fixed/gradual	Up to 25 years	Large debt, need smallest payment
Income-Driven (IDR)	% of income	20-25 years	Unpredictable, lower earnings

Each plan balances cost, speed, and stress differently.

- **Standard** is your "rip the Band-Aid off" approach—finished fastest but with more pressure upfront.
- **Graduated** is the "training wheels" option—easy at first and more challenging later.
- **Extended** is for the long planners—you will pay more overall but have breathing room monthly.
- **IDR** is your financial life jacket, adjusting to what you actually earn and keeping you above water.

Forgiveness Options

Some repayment options can lead to loan forgiveness, meaning the government wipes out what is left after you meet certain criteria. Here is what to know:

- **Public Service Loan Forgiveness (PSLF):** Forgives your remaining balance after 10 years of on-time payments while working for a qualifying government or nonprofit employer. This is great for teachers, nurses, and public-sector workers.
- **Teacher Loan Forgiveness:** Teachers working in low-income schools can qualify for up to $17,500 in forgiveness after five years.
- **IDR Forgiveness:** After 20–25 years of income-driven payments, any remaining balance is forgiven. Just be aware that the forgiven amount could count as taxable income.

I have seen friends breathe literal sighs of relief after qualifying for PSLF. One told me it felt like winning the lottery. The catch is paperwork. You must certify your employment and payments every year to keep your progress valid. Miss a certification and it is like skipping a stamp on your loyalty card; those payments might not count.

Consolidation vs. Refinancing

Once you are juggling multiple loans, you might want to simplify. That is where consolidation and refinancing come in, and they are not the same thing.

Consolidation combines your federal loans into one, with a single monthly payment and a weighted-average interest rate. You keep all the federal perks, such as income-driven plans and forgiveness eligibility. It is mainly about convenience, not savings, but simplicity counts for a lot when you are managing multiple bills.

Refinancing, on the other hand, replaces your federal loans with a new private loan, often at a lower interest rate if you have good credit. It sounds tempting, right? But there is a major catch. Once you refinance, you lose every federal protection. No IDR plans, no forgiveness programs, and no deferment during tough times. It is like trading a safety net for a slightly lower bill.

So, here is the quick rule:

- If all your loans are federal, consolidate if you want easier management.
- If you qualify for forgiveness or IDR, do not refinance. Keep your federal protections.
- Only refinance if your job and income are stable and the interest rate difference is large enough to justify the risk.

Think of consolidation as organizing your closet, and refinancing as selling half your wardrobe to buy a new one. It might look cleaner, but it is a one-way decision.

No matter which plan you pick, remember that repayment is not a lifelong sentence. You can switch plans, adjust payments, or even pause temporarily if life throws you curveballs. The goal is not just to pay it off, but to stay in control without letting debt rule your choices.

It is also worth setting small milestones along the way. Every six months, review your balance and celebrate progress. Even paying an extra $20 now and then makes a visible difference over time. I still remember the first time my loan balance dropped below $10,000; I may have done a small victory dance in my kitchen.

Your repayment plan should fit your life, not the other way around. Start with what you can handle today, and adjust as you grow. Consistency, not perfection, is what builds long-term financial confidence.

Stress-Free Loan Management: Setting Up Automation and Avoiding Missed Payments

The simple truth is: Student loan payments are not anyone's favorite thing to remember. Between work, bills, and the occasional "oops, I forgot rent was due," it is easy for a loan payment to slip through the cracks. The trick is to make repayment feel automatic so you don't have to think about it more than once a month.

The best part? You can set it up in less time than it takes to make a cup of coffee.

Step 1: Automate Everything

Almost every loan servicer lets you set up auto-pay through their website. Look for buttons labeled "Auto Pay" or "Recurring Payments." Once you are logged in, enter your checking account information, choose the day you want your payment to come out, and hit confirm. That is it.

The setup takes about 10 minutes, and it is one of the smartest money moves you can make. When your payment is automated, you will never get hit with a late fee or a credit ding because you got busy or forgot what day it was.

There is also a hidden perk: Many federal and private loan servicers give you a small interest rate discount for enrolling in auto-pay, usually about 0.25%. It might not sound like much, but over the life of a $25,000 loan, it can save you a few hundred dollars. That is money that could go toward groceries, travel, or literally anything more exciting than interest.

Step 2: Time Your Payments Right

Make sure your payment comes out after your paycheck hits your account. This prevents overdrafts and panic. For example, if you are paid on the first of the month, schedule your payment for the eighth or ninth. That gives your paycheck a chance to clear, your bills to settle, and your stress level to stay normal.

If your income changes from month to month, set a calendar reminder a few days before your loan payment date. Open your banking app, make sure you have enough in your account, and relax knowing you are covered.

Step 3: Keep Tabs on Your Loans

Automation does not mean "set it and forget it." It just means you are steering on cruise control instead of driving with your knees.

Every few months, log in to your loan dashboard and check your balance, due date, and interest rate. For federal loans, go to StudentAid.gov and sign in with your FSA ID. You will see every federal loan you have, its servicer, and its progress. Private loans will have their own websites, so make sure you know where each one lives.

A quick check takes five minutes but helps catch errors before they turn into headaches. Occasionally, servicers apply payments incorrectly or mislabel accounts. Spotting an issue early can save you a phone call and a pile of frustration later.

Step 4: Track Your Forgiveness Progress

If you are working toward Public Service Loan Forgiveness (PSLF) or an Income-Driven Repayment (IDR) forgiveness plan, stay organized. Missing a certification or skipping an annual update can delay forgiveness by years.

Use your StudentAid.gov dashboard to track your qualifying payments, confirm that your employer is certified, and download your payment history once or twice a year. It is the digital version of keeping receipts for your future freedom.

One of my friends nearly lost credit for two years of payments because she forgot to resubmit her employment certification. Luckily, she caught it in time, but it was a close call. Her advice: treat it like filing taxes. Put it on your yearly calendar and get it done early.

Step 5: Schedule a Yearly "Loan Checkup"

Pick one date every year to give your student loans a little maintenance check. Tie it to something easy to remember, like your birthday or when you file your taxes. Log in to all your accounts, review your balances, interest rates, and payment history, and make sure your auto-pay is still running smoothly.

If your income has changed or you have a new job, see if a different repayment plan could save you money. You can use the federal Loan Simulator again to compare your current setup with other options. Even a small adjustment could free up $50 or $100 a month, which adds up fast.

I treated my annual checkup like a quick coffee date with my finances. Ten minutes later, I had peace of mind and usually spot one or two small tweaks worth making.

Step 6: Mix Tech With Real Life

Apps like Rocket Money, Undebt.it, or a simple Google Sheet can help you visualize your progress. Some people color-code their balances or make a progress bar for motivation. You can also link your accounts in tools like Monarch Money to watch your balances drop automatically.

Whether you are tech-savvy or prefer pen and paper, the key is awareness. Seeing your balance shrink each month builds motivation and reminds you that every payment matters.

Step 7: Adjust When Life Changes

Got a new job, a raise, or a big move? Log in to your loan servicer and update your income or repayment plan right away. You might qualify for a lower payment or a faster payoff strategy. If money gets tight, ask about switching to an income-driven plan or applying for a temporary pause through deferment or forbearance.

If you ever notice something that seems off, such as a missing payment or an unexpected charge, contact your servicer immediately. Mistakes happen, and catching them early keeps your credit and peace of mind safe.

Final Thoughts

Student loans can feel like a permanent houseguest who never stops asking for rent, but once you set up automation, the noise fades into the background. Combine auto-pay, reminders, and regular check-ins, and your repayment will practically run itself.

With a few smart systems in place, you can stop worrying about missing payments and start focusing on bigger goals. It's no fun obsessing over debt every day. With these steps in place, you can start building quiet confidence that you have everything under control.

And that feeling? That is the real payoff.

What to Do if You're Overwhelmed, Behind, or Facing Hardship

Student loans can feel like that one friend who keeps texting, "Hey, you up?" at the worst possible time. The moment you start to relax, a new bill arrives or another reminder pops up in your inbox. If you have ever felt stressed, behind, or unsure what to do next, you are not alone.

Life happens. Jobs change, rent increases, and sometimes you simply cannot make the payment that month. Do not panic or ignore the situation. Take a breath, stay calm, and start with one small action.

Checking for Help

If making payments feels impossible, the first move is to log in to your loan servicer's website. Most servicers have built-in tools that let you pause or reduce payments when your income changes. Some can even help you switch to a more manageable plan.

Next, pick up the phone and call them. It might feel intimidating, but the fastest path forward is to talk with a real person. Be honest about what is going on and ask them to walk you through your options.

You can start the conversation with something simple like, "Hi, I'm having trouble making my student loan payment right now. Can you explain what options I have for deferment, forbearance, or reduced payments?"

These representatives hear this every day. You do not have to feel embarrassed or ashamed for asking for help.

Deferment and Forbearance

If you need temporary breathing room, you might qualify for deferment or forbearance.

Deferment pauses your payments, and if you have a subsidized federal loan, the government covers the interest while your payments are on hold. Forbearance also pauses payments but allows interest to keep building on all loans.

Both are designed to help during short-term challenges such as unemployment, illness, or major life changes. When applying, you will usually need to explain your situation or provide proof of income loss. Applications are often processed within a couple of weeks, and everything can be done online most of the time.

The goal is to use these tools as a short-term safety net and return to regular payments as soon as possible so that interest does not keep adding up.

Recovering From Missed Payments

If you have already missed several payments or your loan has gone into default, you can still recover. The best option in this situation is usually loan rehabilitation.

Rehabilitation means you agree to make nine on-time, income-based payments over ten months. These payments are often small, sometimes as low as five or ten dollars depending on your income. Once you complete the plan, your loan comes out of default, and the default mark is removed from your credit report.

Defaulting on a loan can lead to wage garnishment, collection calls, and even a seized tax refund. Acting quickly prevents those consequences and helps you rebuild your financial reputation.

Avoiding Common Pitfalls

When people get overwhelmed, it is easy to make choices that back-fire later. Watch out for these common mistakes:

- **Ignoring communication:** Skipping emails or calls from your servicer only makes things worse. They can help if you reach out early.
- **Paying third-party "relief" companies:** If anyone promises to erase your loans for a fee, hang up. These are scams. Always go through your official servicer or StudentAid.gov.
- **Feeling ashamed:** Debt happens. It does not mean you failed. What matters is taking the next step and getting back on track.

When Stress Takes Over

Sometimes, the hardest part of loan trouble is emotional, not financial. It can be draining to see your balance grow or to feel stuck. That is when professional, free support can make a difference. The following resources can help:

- The National Foundation for Credit Counseling (NFCC) offers free, confidential help from certified counselors.
- Your college's financial aid office might have post-graduation advisors who can explain repayment and connect you with nonprofit programs.
- Some local credit unions also host free workshops or one-on-one sessions about repayment planning.

Talking with someone who understands the system can turn confusion into clarity and remind you that you are not facing this alone.

Getting Back on Track

My friend Kenny once ignored his student loans after losing his job. He stopped checking his email because every message felt like bad news. Within a few months, his credit score dropped and late fees piled up. Finally, he called his loan servicer, explained the situation, and learned he qualified for an income-driven plan that dropped his payment to $30 a month.

Within a year, his score started improving, and his stress level dropped. His advice to anyone in the same boat: "Call early, not late. It feels scary, but once you start the conversation, you realize the solution was always easier than you thought."

Perspective and Progress

Falling behind does not define you. Missing payments or entering forbearance does not erase your ability to recover. What matters is taking small, consistent actions that move you forward.

Every payment you make, every phone call you complete, and every login to check your progress counts as a win. Even if it feels slow, you are building momentum.

Student loans can be frustrating, but they do not get to control your story. Once you understand your options and take ownership, you have the power to turn the page and move toward financial freedom.

Fast-Tracking Your Payoff Without Sacrificing Everything Fun

Paying off student loans can feel like standing at the bottom of a mountain with a backpack full of bricks. The good news is that you do not have to sprint to the top or give up everything fun in your life to make real progress. Steady, consistent steps will get you there faster than trying to do it all at once.

The best way to start is with small moves that fit into your current life. Round up your payment each month, even by a little. If you normally pay $210, make it $235 instead. That extra $25 adds up to $300 a year, which cuts down interest and helps you finish sooner. When you get unexpected money, like a tax refund, bonus, or birthday gift, send part of it to your loan. Even one extra payment a year can shorten your repayment timeline.

If you have a side hustle, use it to your advantage. You do not need to add another full-time job. Just find a small source of income that you can dedicate to your debt payments. One friend of mine waited tables on weekends and sent every tip over $10 straight to her student loan. Another picked up freelance design work and funneled half of each project toward her balance. It was not glamorous, but it worked. Small, steady contributions make a huge difference over time.

Technology can help, too. Many banks now offer round-up features that save your spare change from everyday purchases. Buy a coffee for $4.25, and the app rounds it to $5.00, sending the extra 75 cents into a savings bucket. Once it reaches $50 or $100, transfer it toward your loan. It feels like progress without effort. If you use a cash-back credit card, redeem your rewards to pay down debt. Every little bit moves you closer to the finish line.

If you like visual motivation, use tools such as Rocket Money or Undebt.it to track how much you have paid down and how much you save in interest. Watching that number shrink feels rewarding and keeps you focused.

Celebrating Your Wins

Progress deserves celebration. Paying off debt takes time, so enjoy the milestones. Celebrate when you hit the halfway mark, make an extra payment, or finally pay off your smallest loan. It can be something simple like a nice dinner, a night out, or just crossing the number off a chart. A friend of mine threw a small pizza party when she made her final payment. She posted a photo of her shredded loan statement online, and her friends flooded the comments with encouragement. That moment felt like a graduation all over again.

Sharing your wins also keeps you accountable and inspires others. You can post updates, keep a notebook, or use a simple tracker. Watching your progress grow is motivating, especially when you realize how much your effort is paying off.

In no way should paying off student debt mean living without fun. Instead, create habits that let you make progress without feeling deprived. Every small payment counts. Each side gig deposit, each round-up transfer, and each mindful spending choice brings you closer to freedom.

You do not need to rush or give up everything you enjoy. The goal is balance and living your life while building your future. Keep going, stay consistent, and remind yourself that every dollar you pay today is buying back your peace of mind tomorrow. If you are able to put some of this extra money away toward savings, the next chapter will help you with that.

Chapter 7

Saving for Now and Later

Emergency Funds, Goals, and Automation

Creating a "Break Glass" Emergency Fund: How Much and How Fast

You know that gut-dropping moment when your car makes a strange noise, your phone slips onto the sidewalk, or you get a surprise medical bill? That's life reminding you that an emergency fund is not optional. It's your financial airbag, the thing that softens the blow when reality decides to take a swing.

An emergency fund is about these two things: survival and sanity. It's the cushion between you and stress when the unexpected happens. Emergencies include anything urgent and unplanned, like a flat tire, a vet bill, a broken laptop, or an unexpected copay.

I learned the value of an emergency fund the hard way. A few years ago, I was driving to a friend's wedding in another state. I made it to my hotel just fine, but the next morning, my car wouldn't start. The battery had died overnight, and I was hours from home in unfamiliar territory. Between the tow truck, a replacement battery, and the extra time it took to get back on the road, the costs piled up fast. I didn't have an emergency fund then, so everything went on a credit card, and the interest followed me for months. I promised myself that day I'd never let a dead battery ruin both my plans and my finances again. The next year, when my alternator went out, I was ready. I dipped into my emergency fund, paid the bill, and kept going without missing a beat. Same car trouble, completely different peace of mind.

When people hear "three-to-six months of expenses," they often freeze before they start. That amount can sound impossible when you're just getting by. Instead, begin with a small target of $500–1,000. That's enough to turn chaos into inconvenience. It covers things like car repairs, urgent dental work, or replacing a cracked phone screen. Once you hit that first goal, aim for one month of expenses, then gradually build toward three.

Keeping Your Emergency Fund Safe

Keep your emergency fund separate from your everyday money. A high-yield savings account is ideal because it earns more interest and keeps your cash accessible within a day or two. Online banks like Ally or Capital One offer strong rates and easy transfers. Label the account "Break Glass Only" or "Emergency Fund" to remind yourself what it's for. If you know you'll be tempted to dip in, open the account at a different bank so you have to make a conscious effort to move money.

The easiest way to grow your fund is automatically. Schedule a small transfer every payday, even if it's just $10 or $20. You can also use your bank's round-up feature to send spare change from purchases into your savings. Selling unused clothes, books, or gadgets on Depop, OfferUp, or Facebook Marketplace is another quick way to build momentum. Every little bit counts, and seeing that balance rise feels surprisingly rewarding.

Your emergency fund should feel sacred. If you ever think about dipping into it, stop and ask yourself, *Would I still feel okay if a real emergency happened tomorrow?* If the answer is no, don't touch it. Try keeping it in an account without a debit card so it's harder to withdraw impulsively.

Now, grab a notebook or open your notes app and write down three emergencies that could realistically hit you this year, such as a car repair, a medical bill, or a laptop replacement. Estimate the cost of each. Add them up and ask yourself if your savings could cover at least one of them. If not, you've just identified your first savings goal.

Sinking Funds for Life's Little (And Big) Goals

If your emergency fund protects you from life's surprises, sinking funds help you plan for the things you already know are coming. Think of them as mini–savings buckets that take the stress out of predictable expenses. Instead of panicking when big bills or fun opportunities appear, you're ready.

A sinking fund is simple: It's money you set aside regularly for a specific purpose. It could be for car repairs, holiday gifts, or a trip you've been dreaming about. Think of it as a way to spread out costs over time rather than facing one large bill all at once.

Here's how it works. Suppose you want to buy a new $600 laptop six months from now. Instead of charging it to a credit card, divide $600 by six. That's $100 per month, or $25 per week. When the time comes, you can buy it without debt or guilt. The same approach works for car insurance, birthdays, or those recurring expenses that always seem to sneak up when you least expect them.

I started using sinking funds after one too many surprise expenses hit in the same month. I had to renew my car registration, replace two tires, and buy a wedding gift all at once. It completely drained my checking account. After that, I made a list of the big expenses that tend to pop up throughout the year, such as travel, gifts, and annual subscriptions. I began setting aside small amounts each month. Now, when those moments come, the money is already waiting. The stress that used to follow them is gone.

Both emergency funds and sinking funds fit naturally into the budget systems you learned back in Chapter 3. Your emergency fund belongs in your "needs" category because it protects your essential expenses, such as housing, food, and transportation, from future surprises. Sinking funds often land in the "wants" or "savings goals" section of your budget. They cover planned but irregular expenses like vacations, gifts, or annual fees. When you give these savings a spot in your monthly plan, you stop being caught off guard and start feeling in control. Whether you use the 50/30/20 method or a zero-based budget, set aside a small slice of your income for each. Even five percent of your paycheck can be split between these two goals to build real stability over time.

Most banks make it easy to create multiple savings goals within a single account. If your bank offers "buckets" or "envelopes," label each one for your specific goals, such as "Travel," "Car Repairs," or "Holiday Gifts." Move small amounts into each bucket every payday. If your bank doesn't offer this feature, a spreadsheet or budgeting app works just as well. One friend of mine even uses color-coded sticky notes on her mirror to track her goals. Every time she transfers money, she adds a check mark next to that goal. It's simple, visual, and satisfying.

The best part of sinking funds is how effortless they make saving feel. You're not scrambling to cover something last-minute or choosing between fun and responsibility. You're simply preparing in advance. Whether you move $10 toward your next trip or $25 toward new sneakers, each small step makes a big difference later.

My cousin Jess used to dread spring break because she never had enough money saved. One year, she decided to transfer $15 a week starting in January. By March, she had enough for her trip without touching her credit card. Another friend, Curtis, set up a "Tech Upgrade Fund" and slowly saved for a new laptop. When he finally made the purchase, he felt confident and stayed debt-free.

People who use sinking funds consistently say they feel more in control of their finances because they're finally ahead of their expenses instead of constantly catching up. Saving stops feeling like a sacrifice and starts feeling like smart planning for things that actually matter.

It's easy to think, *I'll save for that later*, but "later" usually ends up being expensive. Sinking funds make later easier because you've already prepared for it. Whether it's replacing your tires, traveling home for the holidays, or buying concert tickets the moment they go on sale, you'll have the money ready when you need it.

Emergency Fund vs. Sinking Fund

Category	Emergency Fund	Sinking Fund
Purpose	Only true emergencies	Planned or expected expenses
When to Use	Medical bill, job loss, major repair	Travel, gifts, tech upgrades
Access Frequency	Rarely	Once or twice per year (per goal)
Goal Amount	$500 - 3 months of living expenses	Varies depending on the specific goal

Automating Your Savings: Set It and Forget It

Saving money is a lot easier when you take yourself out of the equation. Willpower sounds great in theory, but after a long day or a tempting sale, it doesn't always show up. That's where automation comes in. It's the simplest way to make saving happen without effort or guilt.

Automation means setting up your accounts so money moves itself. You decide the amount and timing once, and it happens every payday like clockwork. It's the financial version of setting your coffee maker to start before you wake up. You don't have to think about it; you just reap the benefits.

Split Direct Deposit and Automatic Transfers

There are two main ways to automate your savings. The first is through split direct deposit. If your employer allows it, have part of your paycheck sent directly to your savings account and the rest to checking. You can choose a flat amount, such as $50, or a percentage of each paycheck. This is "set it and forget it" saving at its finest because the money is out of sight before you ever have a chance to spend it.

The second method is using your bank's automatic transfer feature. Most banking apps let you set up a recurring transfer from checking to savings. Choose an amount that feels comfortable and schedule it for the same day your paycheck hits. This keeps you saving before you start spending. Even $20 every week adds up faster than you think.

Apps and online banks make this process even easier. Many offer built-in tools that move money automatically based on your habits. You can create "rules" like transferring one dollar every time you buy coffee or rounding up each purchase to the nearest dollar and saving the spare change. It doesn't feel like much, but after a few weeks, those tiny amounts turn into something noticeable. Tools such as Qapital, Digit, or Chime's Save When You Get Paid feature do this automatically, moving small, safe amounts based on your spending patterns.

How to Use Automation

Automation also fits perfectly with the budgeting methods you learned earlier. If you use a zero-based budget, schedule savings transfers right when you plan your month, just like any other bill. If you follow the 50/30/20 method, set your "20% for savings" to move automatically into your chosen accounts. By taking the choice out of your hands, you remove the temptation to skip or delay saving.

If you're worried about overdrafts or an unpredictable income, keep automation flexible. Most apps let you pause, adjust, or skip transfers anytime. You can even set notifications to remind you when the transfer happens so you stay in control. Once you're comfortable, you can increase the amount little by little.

I used to transfer money manually, but I'd forget half the time. After switching to automation, I stopped thinking about saving altogether, and my balance quietly grew every month. The best part was realizing how little I missed the money once it was out of reach. A few months later, I checked my account and couldn't believe how quickly it had built up.

If you have multiple goals, try setting up separate accounts for each—one for your emergency fund, another for sinking funds, and maybe one labeled "Future Fun" for something you're excited about. Giving your savings a name adds purpose and makes it harder to raid the wrong account when temptation hits.

If you want to boost progress, increase your automated transfer by five or ten dollars every few months. It's an effortless way to grow your savings faster. Set a calendar reminder to revisit your setup quarterly, around the same time you review your budget.

Automation turns saving from a task you have to remember into a background process that works. Once it's set up, it keeps you moving toward your goals smoothly and quietly. You'll be amazed at how easy saving feels when it happens automatically, and you don't have to lift a finger.

Surviving Financial Surprises: What to Do When the Unexpected Hits

Even the best budgets get shaken up by the unexpected. You could be cruising through your week when your paycheck is smaller than expected, your roommate forgets their share of rent, or a medical bill appears out of nowhere. These moments feel overwhelming, but with a plan, they don't have to turn into full-blown crises.

When something goes wrong, the first step is to pause and breathe. Panic leads to bad decisions. Start by listing all the bills and expenses due within the next two weeks. Be brutally honest about what's coming up. Then, rank them by importance. Rent, food, and utilities always come first because they keep you safe and stable. After that, focus on minimum payments for loans or credit cards to protect your credit. Anything nonessential, like streaming subscriptions or take-out, can wait until things settle.

If you can't pay everything in full, contact your creditors, landlord, or utility companies right away before payments are late. You'll be surprised how willing most people are to help when you're proactive. A short, honest message can go a long way:

"Hi [Name], I'm facing a temporary setback and wanted to reach out before my payment is due. I can pay [$X] now and the rest by [date]. Is there flexibility with the due date or fees?"

For essential bills, call customer service and ask if they offer payment plans, extensions, or hardship programs. Many companies have them but rarely advertise them. If you're polite and upfront, most will work with you.

Cash Is King

If cash is tight, look at all possible safe sources before turning to credit cards or loans. Check if you have any flexible sinking funds that can be temporarily tapped. You can also sell unused items online for quick cash, like old textbooks, clothes, or electronics. If you have friends or family you trust, a small short-term loan can work if you're clear about the repayment plan. Always write it down and follow through. Protecting the relationship matters as much as the money.

Colleges and employers often offer emergency grants or paycheck advances. Check your school's financial aid office, HR department, or company intranet for programs you might not know exist. Community resources can also help. Local nonprofits, food pantries, or neighborhood groups often provide short-term assistance for rent, utilities, or groceries. I once had a friend who received an unexpected bill and found out her county offered a one-time assistance fund for residents facing hardship. She applied online and got approved within a week.

If you do reach out to creditors or landlords, document every conversation. Write down names, dates, and what was agreed upon. Having a paper trail helps protect you from mix-ups or extra fees later.

And please, avoid payday loans or quick-cash apps that charge high interest. They seem like lifesavers at first, but often create months of new problems. It's better to slow down, communicate honestly, and work with legitimate lenders or service providers than to dig yourself into deeper debt.

Here's a quick checklist for when life throws you a financial curveball:

- Write down every upcoming bill or expense.
- Rank them: rent or mortgage first, then food, then utilities.
- Contact companies before payments are missed and ask for extensions or payment plans.
- Look for safe cash sources, including sinking funds, selling items, or employer programs.
- Reach out to local nonprofits or community groups if needed.
- Document every agreement and payment plan.
- Avoid payday loans or any high-interest borrowing.

Most importantly, remember that everyone hits financial turbulence at some point. It doesn't mean you're bad with money. What matters is how quickly you act and how honest you are with yourself and others. I've had moments when I felt completely stuck, only to realize that asking for help and taking one small step at a time made the problem manageable.

Surviving a financial surprise requires staying calm, thinking clearly, and protecting your essentials first. Once the dust settles, you can rebuild your momentum and strengthen your safety nets so the next surprise feels a little less scary.

Quick-Start Savings Challenges (That Don't Kill Your Social Life)

Saving money doesn't have to feel like punishment. Turning it into a game makes the whole process easier and fun. I've found that when saving feels like a challenge instead of a chore, it's much easier to stay consistent and sometimes even a little competitive.

One of my favorite mini-challenges started with coffee. I realized how much I was spending on drive-through lattes and decided to make my own for just one week. I invited a couple of friends to join in, and we turned it into a contest: who could brew the best "home café" drink and who would give in first. We laughed at the first few disasters, but by the end of the week, I had saved about $30 and actually enjoyed the routine.

If coffee isn't your weakness, try the "round-up challenge." For 30 days, every debit or credit card purchase gets rounded up to the next dollar, and the extra change goes straight into savings. Watching those small amounts grow feels surprisingly satisfying. Or set a simple rule: no online shopping until payday. You'll be amazed at how many "urgent" carts don't feel so important after a few days.

Cash lovers can take the "No Five-Dollar Bill" approach. Every time you get a five, tuck it into a jar and forget about it until the end of the month. If you're more of a numbers person, try the 30-day incremental challenge: Save one dollar on day one, two dollars on day two, and so on until day thirty. You'll have $465 by the end without really feeling the pinch.

Another favorite is the "Cancel and Save" challenge. Pick one subscription you rarely use, cancel it, and automatically transfer that monthly cost into your savings account instead. It's guilt-free progress, and you might never miss the app.

If you like a little friendly competition, get friends or roommates involved. Everyone can chip in ten dollars a week to a shared savings pot and agree to a fun group reward at the end, such as dinner out, a movie night, or bragging rights for the biggest saver. Tracking your progress together keeps motivation high and makes the process social instead of solitary.

Whatever challenge you choose, make sure to celebrate the win. Track your savings in your notes app or print a simple progress chart. When you hit your goal, reward yourself with something small, like a favorite meal, a new book, or a guilt-free night out. Try to recognize that saving money is about consistency, not perfection.

These small challenges build powerful habits. They prove that saving can fit into real life, even when you're busy or on a tight budget. Each win gives you a little more confidence and control over your money. And once you see how those tiny steps add up, you'll be ready to move from saving to growing, which moves us into the next chapter, which is all about investing and turning progress into long-term wealth.

Chapter 8

Investing for Beginners

Growing Your Money, One Step at a Time

Why Invest Now: Compound Interest and "Future You"

I f you have ever wondered how some people your age already have investment accounts quietly growing in the background, the secret usually is not luck or a giant inheritance. They simply started early, invested tiny amounts, and let time do most of the heavy lifting. The real magic behind this is compound interest, one of the few financial forces that is both simple and almost suspiciously powerful.

Compound interest works like this: You put in a little money, it grows, and then that growth starts to earn more growth. Your returns earn returns. Over time, it snowballs. The earlier you start, the more time that snowball has to roll downhill and turn into something impressive instead of a sad little ice chunk.

Here is an example. If you invest $25 a month starting at age 20, you will contribute a total of $12,000 by age 60. With a typical 7% yearly return, that can grow to more than $60,000. Wait until age 30 to start, and the same $25 per month might only grow to around $29,000. The only difference is time. Starting earlier is like getting the good seat at a concert. Every minute counts.

Start Age	Invest/Month	Invested by 60	Grows to
20	$25	$12,000	$60,000+
30	$25	$9,000	$29,000+

You do not need a lot of money to invest. You just need to begin. As little as $5, $10, or even the leftover change from your morning coffee can grow into something meaningful when you give it enough years. Time is doing most of the work anyway. You are just giving it something to work with.

Here is another snapshot of the power of early investing. A single $100 investment at age 20 can grow to more than $1,500 by age 60. $5,000 invested at 20 could become nearly $75,000. That is the closest thing to a financial cheat code most of us will ever get.

Amount Invested	Approx. Value at 60
$100	$1,500
$500	$7,500
$1,000	$15,000
$2,500	$37,400
$5,000	$74,900

But investing is not just about numbers. It is about what future you gets to enjoy. Maybe it is travel, a reliable car, a nicer apartment, or simply peace of mind. One of my friends set up a $40 monthly automatic investment during college. He barely noticed it leaving his account. By graduation, he had enough saved to take a trip to Thailand with money left over.

If investing still feels intimidating, start tiny. You can invest $5 or $10 using apps that make everything simple. Link your bank account, choose a recurring amount, and let the app do the rest. Rounding-up tools make it even easier. Buy something for $3.75, and the app invests the extra 25 cents. Little amounts add up fast, kind of like how your laundry pile grows even when you swear you did it yesterday.

Quick Interactive: Visualize Your Future Money

Take 30 seconds and picture something future you would be excited about. It might be a vacation, a laptop upgrade, or the deposit for your first apartment. Then answer:

1. What small amount can I invest each month without noticing it?
2. How much would that amount grow over 10 or 20 years?

Use a free compound-interest calculator and plug in your numbers. Seeing the potential makes investing feel a lot less mysterious and a lot more motivating.

Investing does not require perfection or becoming a financial expert. You're creating options for your future self. Even a few dollars per paycheck is enough to begin. The first step is the most important one, and once you take it, your money starts quietly working for you while you go live your life.

Basic Investment Options: What Young Adults Need to Know

Investing looks complicated from the outside, but once you understand the basics, it stops feeling like a secret money club. The three core building blocks for young investors are stocks, bonds, and IRAs. Learn how each one works, and everything becomes much easier.

Stocks, Bonds, and IRAs

Stocks are tiny pieces of ownership in companies. If you buy a share of a company like Apple, you literally own a small piece of it. As the company grows, your piece can grow in value, too. You might even earn dividends, which are like a little thank-you payment for being an owner. Stocks can bounce around a lot from day to day, but over longer periods, they usually grow more than money sitting in a regular savings account.

Bonds work differently. When you buy a bond, you are lending money to a company or the government. They agree to pay you interest and return your original money at the end of the loan period. Bonds tend to move up and down less than stocks. Think of stocks as the busy, unpredictable part of your financial team and bonds as the steady coworker who always shows up on time and keeps everyone calm.

Most beginners do not want to spend their free time researching individual companies, and the good news is that they do not have to. Index funds and ETFs do the work for you. These are collections of many companies wrapped into one investment. For example, an S&P 500 index fund gives you a slice of 500 different companies at once. That way, your success does not depend on picking one winning company. If a few companies stumble, the others help keep your investment moving.

Many young adults open their first investments through IRAs. IRA stands for individual retirement account, and it is basically a special container built to help your money grow over time with tax advantages. There are two main types: traditional and Roth. You choose based on when you want your tax break. A traditional IRA might reduce your taxes today, while a Roth IRA gives you tax-free withdrawals later. Since many young adults are in a lower tax bracket now than they will be later in life, the Roth IRA usually delivers the bigger long-term benefit.

Here's a quick comparison:

Feature	Roth IRA	Traditional IRA
Taxes Now?	Yes (on contributions)	No (may be deducted)
Taxes Later?	No (withdrawals are tax-free)	Yes (pay when withdrawing)
Early Access?	Contributions can be withdrawn	Penalties apply before age 59 1/2
Best for	Young adults/low earners	High earners now

Choosing the right type of IRA is only the first step. Once the account is open, you still need to choose your investments. Many young investors stick with a simple index fund or ETF because it is easy to understand and proven to work well over long time periods. After that, automatic contributions help your account grow without much effort. Even $10 or $20 per paycheck adds up when you invest it regularly.

Try to ignore the noise from friends or social media "influencers" who brag about fast profits or overnight wins. That type of investing often comes with unnecessary risk. Slow and steady is a much better approach, especially in the beginning. You do not have to watch the stock market every day or get caught up in dramatic headlines. Investing is more about patience than excitement.

Stocks help your money grow, bonds help keep things steady, index funds make investing simple, and IRAs add tax benefits that make your future self very happy. Once you understand these pieces, you will see that you do not need to be an expert to become a confident long-term investor. Your goal should be progress and consistency over time.

How to Start Investing With $50 (Using Apps You Already Have)

You do not need a finance degree, a Wall Street mentor, or a stack of cash to start investing. If you can pull together $50 from a birthday card, a side gig, or skipping delivery for a week, you have everything you need. The process is far less intimidating than it sounds.

Start by choosing an investing app. Robinhood, Fidelity, and Acorns are all beginner-friendly and quick to set up. Download the app, tap Sign Up, and answer the basic questions it asks. It will want your name, address, date of birth, and Social Security number. This is normal and required by law, even if you are only investing the spare change in your car's cup holder.

Next, the app will ask a few questions about your income, goals, and experience with investing. Do not stress over these because there are no wrong answers. They help the platform make recommendations, not judge your financial worthiness. After that, link your bank account through a secure service like Plaid or connect a debit card. Transfers usually take a day or two to show up.

Once the money arrives, you can invest even tiny amounts. Most apps now offer fractional shares, which means you can invest one dollar into companies or funds that normally cost hundreds. A simple starting point is an S&P 500 ETF. It gives you exposure to 500 companies in one click. Search for VOO or SPY, choose Buy, select Fractional, and enter any amount you want.

It is surprisingly satisfying to see your first trade go through. A friend once used Acorns round-ups on her morning coffee habit and ended the year with more than $80 invested without thinking about it. Sometimes the smallest steps create the best momentum.

Before you invest, the app will give you two choices for account type: a regular taxable account or an IRA.

Here is the simple version:

Account Type	Withdraw Anytime?	Tax Benefits	Best for
Taxable Account	Yes	None	Flexible goals
Roth IRA	Contributions	Tax-free growth/withdrawal	Retirement, long-term
Traditional IRA	No (before 59 1/2)	Deduct now, pay taxes later	Retirement only

A taxable account is flexible. You can add or withdraw money anytime with no age limits or penalties. You will owe taxes on any profits, but the freedom makes it ideal for short-term goals.

A Roth IRA is a retirement account with major tax perks. You can withdraw the money you contributed at any time without penalties. For example, if you contributed $1,000 and it grew to $1,200, you could withdraw the original $1,000 with no penalty. Since most young adults are in a low tax bracket, the Roth IRA is usually the smarter long-term choice.

A Traditional IRA might lower your taxes now, but you cannot withdraw the money before retirement without penalties. This option works better for older adults or higher earners.

If you are not sure which type to choose, it is perfectly fine to start with a regular taxable account. You can always add a Roth IRA later once you are comfortable.

Common snags like Pending Approval messages or slow transfers are normal. Sometimes the app needs a clearer photo of your ID. If you are unsure what to invest in, choose a broad index fund or ETF. They are low-cost, low-stress, and widely recommended for beginners.

The most important step is starting. Warren Buffett said it best: "The best time to invest was yesterday. The second-best time is today." You do not need to wait for perfect timing or perfect knowledge. Start with $5, learn the process, and build from there.

Once you place that first order, even if it is only a few dollars, you are officially an investor. Your money is no longer sitting still. It is out there working for your future, one small step at a time.

Risk, Rewards, and Avoiding Beginner Investing Mistakes

Investing always involves ups and downs, and if you are new to it, the whole experience can feel like a roller coaster. It is exciting on the way up and stomach-dropping on the way down. Think of risk like levels in a video game. Some levels are calm and predictable; others are chaotic and throw surprises at you when you least expect. Stocks usually sit at the wildest levels. They can climb quickly but can also fall sharply when the market gets nervous. Bonds are more relaxed and steady. If stocks are the roller coaster, bonds are the quiet ride through the park. Keeping money in cash is the safest move, but it barely grows and loses value over time to inflation.

Here is a quick comparison of how these choices behave over 10 years:

Asset	Best Case (10 yrs)	Average (10 yrs)	Worst Case (10 yrs)
Stocks	High Rewards	Solid Growth	Sharp losses
Bonds	Modest Growth	Steady Returns	Slight gains/losses
Cash	Barely Grows	Loses to inflation	No real growth

That up-and-down movement is called volatility. It is a normal part of investing, even though it does not feel great when your account balance dips. Headlines make it worse. The louder the news shouts about "market drops" or "investor panic," the more you might feel like you should pull your money out immediately.

But, honestly, even the experts cannot predict every swing in the market. What matters far more is how you handle those swings. The worst thing most new investors do is panic sell. A drop feels scary, so they hit Sell to avoid losing more. But selling while your account is down locks in the loss. Most markets recover with time, and the people who stay invested often end up in a better place than those who try to dodge dips.

Then there is chasing trends. Maybe you see friends bragging on social media about a stock that doubled last month, or someone claims they found the next big crypto coin. FOMO makes you want to jump in, but late arrivals often get caught buying at the top. A friend of mine once bought a hyped-up stock because a viral post said it was going to the moon. One week later, it crashed. He sold in frustration and swore off investing for months. The lesson is simple: Ignore hype and focus on your plan.

To show how important mindset is, here is a story about two very different reactions to a market drop.

Chris had been investing a little each month in a broad index fund. When the market suddenly dropped, he panicked. His account balance fell quickly, and he sold everything to avoid losing more. By the time the market recovered, he had already missed the rebound. Months later, he reinvested carefully, but he knew he had lost real growth simply because he had reacted emotionally.

Emily took the opposite approach. She set up automatic investments and decided from day one that she was in it for the long run. When the same market drop hit, her account dipped too, but she stayed calm. She even joked that everything was on sale. The shares she bought during the downturn were the ones that grew fastest during the recovery. Her steady mindset paid off.

And I will add this from my own experience. I used to be like Chris. The first time the market dropped, I panicked and sold everything. Then I did it again during another decline, even though I already knew the market moves upward over long periods. Eventually, I stopped reacting to every drop, set up automatic investing, and trusted the long-term path. It wasn't easy to keep my emotions in check, but that shift helped me lessen stress and stay invested through ups and downs.

These experiences highlight one big truth: Risk is not the enemy. Emotional reactions are.

Diversification: Finding the Perfect Mix

Diversification is another key way to manage risk. It simply means not placing all your money in one place. Think of your investments like a balanced meal. You want different ingredients, so one disappointing part does not ruin everything else. Your portfolio might mix stocks, bonds, and even international investments. That variety helps reduce how often your account swings wildly.

Here is a simple example of a balanced beginner portfolio:

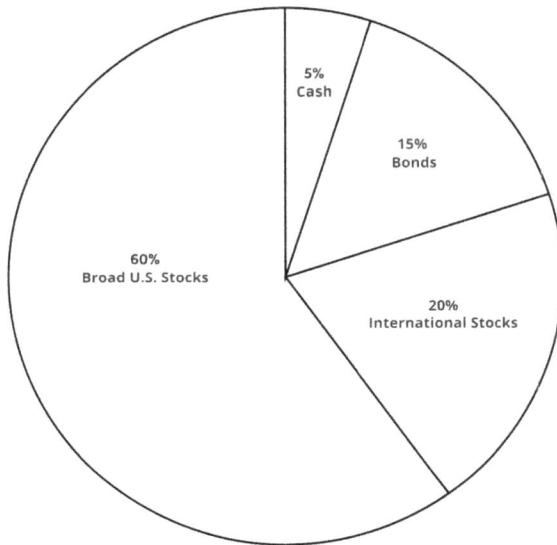

5%
Cash

15%
Bonds

60%
Broad U.S. Stocks

20%
International Stocks

Market swings are guaranteed, but letting them control your decisions is not. When you feel anxious, try zooming out. Look at the last five or ten years instead of the last five or ten days. Most successful investors do not obsess over daily numbers. They focus on consistent contributions that build over time.

Here is a simple list to keep in mind:

Do

- Invest regularly, even small amounts
- Diversify across several types of investments
- Look long term and ignore the daily noise

Do Not

- Panic sell during dips
- Chase trends you do not understand
- Put everything into one company or a risky idea

Mistakes will happen. After all, even seasoned investors slip up sometimes. What matters is learning to stay calm, stay invested, and stay focused on the long run. When you manage risk with patience and smart habits, investing becomes much less stressful and far more rewarding.

Setting Your First Investment Goal: A Simple, Actionable Plan

The first step in investing is not picking stocks or choosing the perfect app. The real starting point is deciding what you want your money to actually do. Without a clear purpose, it is easy to lose focus, get discouraged, or panic the moment the market wiggles. Before anything else, ask yourself: *Why am I investing?* Your answer might be simple: an apartment deposit, a new laptop, a used car, or just a cushion so life feels less stressful. Your goal only has to matter to you.

Take a moment to make your goal specific. Instead of saying "I want to save more," try something like "I want $1,000 for an apartment deposit in two years." Specific goals are easier to work toward because they give you a target and a timeline. If you want that $1,000 in two years, that is about $42 per month or $10 per week. If that feels out of reach, no worries. Start smaller and increase your contribution when you can. Building the habit matters more than hitting the perfect number on day one.

You do not need a fancy calculator to run the math, although online compound interest calculators can help you see different scenarios. If you want a quick example, investing consistently for three years at a seven-percent annual return could look like this:

Contribution	Total Invested (3 yrs)	Possible Value After 3 Years
$10/week	$1,560	$1,690+
$50/month	$1,800	$1,950+

The numbers might seem small now, but consistency turns small choices into real results.

Once your goal feels clear, set up automatic investing. Nearly every platform has an auto-invest or recurring deposit option. Pick an amount, choose weekly or monthly, and let the system do the work. Even $5 a week grows over time when you stay consistent. Automation takes willpower out of the equation. Money moves before you can talk yourself out of it.

At first, it might feel slow. You may look at your account and think, *Seriously, that is it?* Trust the process. After a couple of months, you will start to see momentum. One friend told me her early investments felt like "Monopoly money," but once she saw her balance grow even a little, she was hooked. Another friend shared screenshots of his progress with our group chat, which motivated the rest of us to get started.

If you ever feel embarrassed about starting small, remind yourself that everyone begins somewhere. Your first $100 invested is a big milestone. Celebrate it. Share your progress if you want to. You never know who else you might influence.

And if life gets messy and you need to pause contributions for a while, that is normal. Just restart when you are ready. You are building a lifelong habit, not racing anyone.

Mini-Worksheet: What Am I Investing For?

Before you start sending money into the market, get clear on what you want it to do for you. Use these questions to turn a vague idea into a goal with direction and a plan:

- What's my goal?
- How much do I need?
- By when?
- How much can I set aside each week or month?
- What will reaching this goal allow me to do?

Use this now or save it for later when you are ready to commit.

The truth is simple: Investing works best when you have consistent habits tied to goals that matter to you. Every automatic transfer is a vote for your future self. And now that your money finally has a job and is reporting for duty, the next step is making sure it does not wander off or get derailed by life's chaos. In the next chapter, we will cover how to protect your progress so your hard-earned dollars stay exactly where you want them.

Chapter 9

Dodging Traps

Fraud, Scams, and High-Interest Hazards

Spotting Scams: Red Flags in Apps, Texts, and Emails

Your phone buzzes at 7:13 a.m. with a text from a number you do not recognize: "URGENT: Your bank account has been locked due to unusual activity. Tap this link to verify your identity." Half-awake, you panic. What if you cannot pay rent or use your payment apps today? This fake urgency is exactly how scammers get people to act before thinking. Even tech-savvy young adults fall for these tricks, especially when stressed or overwhelmed by notifications that look real.

Being raised in a digital world does not make you immune to scams. In fact, adults ages 18–59, including Gen Z, are 34% more likely to report losing money to fraud than adults 60 and older, according to the Federal Trade Commission. You use Zelle, buy coffee with your phone, reply to job DMs, and join online giveaways, so scammers tailor their attacks to your habits. They pose as real businesses, mimic bank alerts, and send messages that look identical to the ones you trust.

Phishing is the most common tactic. Emails show up with familiar bank logos but suspicious addresses like "sec-support@bancsecuri1-ty.com." Texts claim your Zelle transfer failed and urge you to log in through a sketchy link. Some malicious apps even copy real icons and interfaces so well that the difference is only visible after the damage is done. Scammers DM you pretending to be influencers, friends, or companies running giveaways. Once you send money, they vanish, usually faster than your roommate when it is their turn to take out the trash.

Common Scams to Watch Out For

Here are everyday scams young adults run into, plus how to spot them:

- **Fake bank alerts:** Scammers text or email you pretending to be your bank, claiming your account is locked or compromised.

How to spot it: The link looks wrong, the message feels urgent, and the sender address is suspicious or slightly misspelled.

- **Zelle, Cash App, or PayPal payment failures:** Messages claim a transfer did not go through and ask you to "confirm your account."

How to spot it: Your real payment app will never ask you to log in through a text message link.

- **Job-offer scams:** A "recruiter" messages you with an easy remote job, then asks for your bank details for "direct deposit."

How to spot it: Real employers never ask for banking info before paperwork. And no job pays $40 an hour to "manage packages from home."

- **Social media giveaways:** An account that looks like a verified influencer asks you to "confirm your identity" with card info or sends you a link to claim a prize.

How to spot it: Real giveaways announce winners publicly and never ask for banking information.

- **Student-loan forgiveness scams:** Messages promise instant loan cancellation for a fee or ask for your Social Security number.

How to spot it: Legit programs use government websites, never Instagram DMs.

- **Friend-in-trouble messages:** A scammer pretends to be someone you know, claiming they lost their wallet or need emergency money.

How to spot it: Ask them to voice call or share a detail only your real friend would know. Scammers usually disappear when questioned.

Scammers thrive on pressure. *"Act now!" "Ten minutes to verify!" "Your account will be closed!"* That type of urgency is the biggest red flag of all.

Whenever a suspicious message comes in, make it a habit to pause before reacting. Check the sender's spelling, look at the link, and ask yourself whether this seems out of the ordinary. If you have doubts, go directly to your bank's official app or website instead of tapping anything in the message. Call the number on the back of your bank card, not the one in the notification.

If an app asks for permissions it should not need, like contacts, messages, or camera access for something simple, delete it. If someone pressures you to act fast, step back and say, *"I need time to verify this."* Legitimate businesses will not object.

Your best tools are caution, a few seconds of pause, and a habit of double-checking anything that feels off. Trust your instincts. If something seems strange, too urgent, or too good to be true, it probably is.

Identity Theft: How to Guard Your Info and What to Do if You're Hit

Identity theft sounds like something that happens to adults dealing with mortgages and tax forms, not young adults scrolling on their phones at midnight. But thieves actually love targeting people under age 25. Your credit history is thin, your guard is down, and you probably use more websites and apps in a week than your parents do all year. That combo makes you an easy target if you are not careful.

Most identity theft starts quietly, which is what makes it so sneaky. It is not some criminal mastermind picking a lock with lasers and orchestral music playing in the background. It is usually something boring, like logging into public Wi-Fi at a coffee shop or tossing out a mail offer without shredding it. Thieves take whatever bits of information they can get. With enough pieces, they can drain your bank account, open credit cards in your name, rent an apartment, or rack up medical bills you will not see until it is too late.

Social media is one of the biggest goldmines for identity thieves. You might think your posts show only your brunch photos and gym selfies, but they also reveal things like your birthday, school, hometown, and even pet names. Those just happen to be the exact questions banks use for account recovery. You do not need to vanish from the internet, but tightening your privacy settings helps a lot. Make your accounts private, clean up who follows you, and skip those "What is your first pet's name" quizzes that are really just free data collection for scammers.

The Importance of Strong Passwords

Weak passwords make things even easier for thieves. If your password is something like "Summer2025" or you use the same password everywhere, you are basically leaving your digital front door open with a welcome sign. Using long, strong, unique passwords is essential. Password managers like 1Password, Bitwarden, or LastPass can create and store everything for you. The only password you need to remember is your master one, which you should write down and store somewhere safe, not in your Notes app labeled "Super Secret Passwords."

Offline risks are real, too. Thieves still dig through trash for bank statements, medical bills, and pre-approved credit card offers. Anything with your name, address, or Social Security number should be shredded or ripped up and tossed in different bags. Yes, it feels dramatic, but it beats spending months fixing a mess someone else created.

Since identity theft often happens silently, your best defense is watching for early warning signs. If you start getting letters about new credit cards you never applied for, calls from debt collectors about accounts you never opened, or emails saying *"Welcome to your new loan,"* do not ignore them. Something is off.

Free apps like Credit Karma or the Experian mobile app can send alerts whenever someone tries to open new credit in your name. Once a year, check your full credit reports at AnnualCreditReport.com. It is free, and it is one of the easiest ways to catch identity theft before the damage gets worse.

Here is a real story. A friend of mine once got a letter congratulating her on her new store credit card from a retailer she had never once shopped at. Whoever stole her info went shopping on her name and credit. She spent weeks calling the bank and the store, filing reports, freezing accounts, and cleaning up the mess. It eventually got fixed, but she did not sleep well for a month.

And here is my experience, though, fortunately, a much easier one to deal with. I once spotted an unfamiliar credit card account on my credit report while doing a routine check. It was clearly not mine. Luckily, I caught it before anyone used it. I contacted the credit bureau right away, had the account closed, and placed alerts on my report. It was a close call, but catching it early prevented bigger problems down the road.

Attacking Identity Theft

If identity theft ever hits you, the most important thing is to act quickly so the damage stays small. Start by placing a fraud alert with one of the major credit bureaus. This tells lenders to slow down and double-check anyone trying to open an account in your name. If you want even stronger protection, freeze your credit entirely. A credit freeze blocks all new accounts from being opened unless you personally lift it.

I have done this and completely forgot about it. I was interviewing for a new job once, and during the routine background check, they told me they could not access my credit file because it was frozen. For a split second, I panicked, then I realized the system was doing exactly what it was supposed to do. I lifted the freeze, the check went through, and I walked away feeling oddly proud of my past self for locking things down.

Next, file a report at IdentityTheft.gov. It guides you step by step, helps you create an official recovery plan, and provides documentation you can use when disputing fraudulent accounts. Save every email, case number, and letter you receive. Then call your bank using the number on your card or their official website. Close compromised accounts, request replacements, and follow their instructions to protect your funds.

Even after things seem resolved, stay alert. Scammers sometimes circle back after a few months when they think you have moved on. Check your bank statements weekly and your credit report monthly until you are confident everything is clean.

Protecting your identity is a mix of online habits and offline awareness. Use strong passwords, keep your profiles private, shred sensitive mail, and monitor your credit regularly. Even if something goes wrong, reacting quickly makes the difference between a stressful day and a financial disaster.

Identity theft is not a personal failure. It happens to countless smart, careful people. What matters most is how quickly you respond and how well you protect yourself going forward.

Payday Loans, Buy Now Pay Later, and Other High-Interest Pitfalls

If you have ever walked past a payday loan shop or seen a flashy ad for instant cash, you know how tempting they can sound when money is tight. Need rent? Need a car repair? Need your laptop fixed right before finals? These places promise quick relief. But behind the neon signs and friendly slogans is one of the most expensive financial traps young adults fall into.

Payday loans are the worst offenders. Borrow $300, and they might charge a $50 fee due in two weeks. That might not seem terrible at first, until you realize that $50 covers only 14 days. If you cannot pay it back immediately, you roll it over and pay another $50. Do that for six months, and you have paid $650 in fees just to borrow $300. That works out to an annual percentage rate of more than 400%. Even high-interest credit cards look friendly compared to that.

Check-cashing stores are not much better. They will cash your paycheck instantly, but for a fee of 2–10% every single time. That adds up quickly. Over a year, you could lose hundreds of dollars that could have gone toward bills, savings, or something fun. The convenience they advertise comes at a very steep price.

Then there are Buy Now Pay Later (BNPL) apps like Klarna, Afterpay, and Affirm. These are everywhere online, especially when you are shopping for clothes, tech, or impulse buys that magically appear in your cart at 1:00 a.m. The pitch sounds harmless. Split a $100 purchase into four $25 payments with no interest if you pay on time. But miss a payment, and you are hit with a $7 or $10 late fee. Miss multiple payments across multiple BNPL purchases, and suddenly, you are juggling fees like a circus performer who has no idea how to juggle.

A friend bought a pair of sneakers using BNPL, then another item, then another. He figured it was only $25 at a time. But he lost track of the due dates and ended up with $40 in late fees in one month. That was more than the original shipping costs he was trying to avoid. Suddenly, that easy four-payment plan did not feel so easy.

These services thrive on urgency, stress, and the hope that you are too overwhelmed to read the fine print. The good news is that you have safer options when money is tight.

How to Protect Yourself

Start by being honest with whoever you owe. Landlords, utility companies, and phone carriers often offer hardship plans or payment extensions if you call before the bill is due. It might feel awkward, but I promise they have heard much worse stories. A quick, respectful call can save you late fees and stress.

If that does not fix things, a small loan from family or a trusted friend with clear repayment expectations written down can be far cheaper than payday loans. Colleges and many employers also offer emergency grants, short-term loans, or paycheck advances. Most students do not realize these programs exist until someone points them out.

I have never taken a payday loan, but I have come close during stressful moments when fast cash felt like the only solution. But every time I stopped and thought about it, the same question hit me hard. If I could not afford my bills now, why would I think I could afford even more later, especially with massive fees attached? That simple thought kept me from jumping into a cycle that would have made everything worse, not better.

To protect yourself, watch out for these red flags:

- Fees required before you receive the loan
- No clear explanation of interest rates or penalties
- Instant approval with zero questions asked
- Pressure to act immediately or sign on the spot
- No official customer service line or physical address
- Vague or missing repayment terms
- Promises that sound too easy or too quick

If you see any of these signs, pause. Take a breath. Remind yourself that easy money is rarely easy and almost never cheap.

When life gets stressful and someone offers a quick financial fix, slow down and look closely. There are always better options than falling into high-interest debt that lingers for months. A little patience, a little communication, and a little planning can save you a lot of money and headaches in the future.

Protecting Your Money: Security Tools and Best Practices

Most of your financial life now lives inside your phone. Your bank, your payment apps, your shopping accounts, even that one food-delivery app you swear you are deleting soon. It is all there. Which is why it always amazes me how many people protect their phone with the same password strength as a middle-school diary. Seriously, if your lock screen code is 1111 or your birthday, please change it before you finish reading this paragraph.

Modern scams do not always look like a guy in a ski mask stealing your wallet. Sometimes the thief is a stranger guessing your weak password, sneaking into your email, or connecting to the same coffee shop Wi-Fi you are using. A few small habits can spare you a huge headache.

Good Security Habits

Start with multi-factor authentication (MFA). MFA is one of the easiest, strongest defenses you can add. If your bank or payment app lets you require a text code, fingerprint, or face scan when you log in, turn it on. Right now. It is like adding a second lock to your front door. Even if someone figures out your password, they still cannot get in without your physical device. If your app lets you use biometrics, take the free upgrade. A hacker can steal a password, but it is a lot harder to steal your face.

Next up is your phone itself. Set it to auto-lock after 30 or 60 seconds. If it ever gets lost or stolen, this small setting gives you a huge advantage. And make sure you have the ability to wipe your device remotely. Apple's Find My and Google's Find My Device let you erase everything with one tap. Think of it as an emergency self-destruct button, except far less dramatic and far more responsible.

Keep your phone and apps updated. I know software updates are annoying, but those updates patch real security holes that hackers love to exploit. Turning on automatic updates saves you from the *"I'll do it later"* routine that never actually happens. My personal rule is simple. If my phone tells me to update, I do it before I forget and get distracted by my fantasy football team.

Public Wi-Fi is another weak spot. Yes, it is convenient, but it is usually about as secure as an unlocked bike. If you must do something sensitive, like checking your bank account, switch to your phone's data instead. Public Wi-Fi is fine for browsing memes, but not for logging in to financial accounts. Save the important stuff for a secure connection.

Another habit that protects you more than you realize is turning on transaction notifications. Your bank and most payment apps let you set alerts for every purchase, no matter how small. Yes, even your $5 iced coffee can trigger a ping. These alerts act like tiny guard dogs. If anything odd happens, you will know immediately. And if you see a charge you do not recognize, you can freeze your card before any real damage is done.

Finally, do a quick weekly check of all your accounts. It takes less than five minutes. Scroll through your recent transactions and make sure everything looks right. If something seems strange, contact your bank using the number on the back of your card. Not the number in a text. Not the number in an email. The real one. This one habit can save you from bigger problems later.

Security Checklist: Make It Routine

- Multi-factor authentication is turned on for every financial account.
- Biometric logins are enabled where possible.
- Auto-lock is set to under one minute.

- Remote wipe is activated on your device.
- Device encryption is turned on.
- Automatic updates are enabled.
- Public Wi-Fi is avoided for anything involving money.
- Transaction alerts are turned on.
- Quick weekly reviews are taken of all accounts.
- Strong, unique passwords are created for every login.

Treat this list like brushing your teeth. It is quick, routine, and prevents long-term problems you definitely do not want.

All of these steps take a few minutes to set up, but they protect you from a lot of stress later. Digital safety does not have to be overwhelming or complicated. You are simply making your financial life harder to break into than the next person's. And in the world of cybersecurity, "harder than the next person" is usually enough to make scammers move on.

What to Do if You've Been Scammed: Immediate Steps for Damage Control

Realizing you have been scammed hits fast. Your heart jumps, your stomach drops, and your mind starts racing. In moments like this, acting quickly really matters. The faster you respond, the better your chances of recovering money, stopping unauthorized activity, and shutting scammers out of your accounts. Take a breath. You are not the first person this has happened to, and you will not be the last. What matters most is what you do next.

- **Alert** your bank or credit card company first. Contact them using the number on their official website or the back of your card. Tell them what happened and ask them to freeze your account, block your card, or reverse any fraudulent transactions. If the scam happened through Venmo, Zelle, or Cash App, report it inside the app and reach out to their support teams. Acting quickly here dramatically improves the odds of stopping further damage.

- **Secure** your accounts next. Change the passwords for anything connected to the scam, especially if you used the same password across different sites. Think email, banking, social media, and shopping accounts. Create strong, unique passwords for each one. A password manager can generate and safely store them for you. Scammers often try stolen login details on multiple sites, hoping you reused them.
- **Report** what happened once your accounts are locked down. File a complaint with the Federal Trade Commission at ReportFraud.ftc.gov. If the scam occurred online, file with the Internet Crime Complaint Center at ic3.gov. For larger losses or safety concerns, notify your local police department. If you are a student, alert your campus IT or security office so they can warn others. These reports help protect both you and your community.

Do not deal with it alone. Tell someone you trust. A friend of mine once got hit with a fake tech-support pop-up and felt embarrassed for days. Once he told his bank and a close friend, he realized he was far from alone. Even professionals fall for convincing scams. You are not the first, and you will not be the last.

- **Monitor** everything for the next few weeks. Review your bank and credit card statements for unfamiliar charges. Set up fraud alerts with Equifax, Experian, and TransUnion, so lenders double-check before opening new accounts in your name. Save every document from your bank, the FTC, or law enforcement. Keep a note with dates, who you spoke to, and what they said. Staying organized helps if you need to follow up later.
- **Reflect** once things have settled. A scam can shake your confidence, but it does not define you. Look at what

142

happened and update your habits to protect yourself moving forward. Maybe you strengthen your passwords, delete sketchy apps, or finally enable multi-factor authentication. Every improvement you make now is a long-term win.

Recovering from a scam is not just about money. It is about regaining control. And the more confident you become in protecting yourself, the easier it gets to speak up, ask questions, and advocate for your financial well-being. All of that matters because your next big skill set includes communicating clearly, setting boundaries, and making sure your voice is heard. That is what we will tackle next as you level up your money confidence in the next chapter.

Chapter 10

Leveling Up

Communication, Advocacy, and Lifelong Money Skills

Money Talks: Scripts for Rent-Splitting, Bill-Busting, and Awkward Conversations

Talking about money with roommates, friends, or family can feel like navigating a minefield while pretending everything is normal. You are sitting in the kitchen on a perfectly good morning, a half-finished container of lo mein on the counter, when your group chat erupts because the Wi-Fi died again. Someone still has not paid their share of the bill, another person claims they "forgot" about the electric payment, and suddenly, you are the one wondering whether you should say something or hope the problem magically fixes itself. Most young adults never learned how to have these conversations without feeling awkward or stressed.

Sharing expenses is part of adult life, but no one wants to be the person constantly chasing payments or reminding everyone about deadlines. At the same time, keeping quiet only leads to resentment, late fees, and group chats filled with passive-aggressive emojis. The good news is that these conversations do not have to be dramatic. With a few simple approaches, you can keep things calm, clear, and way less awkward than you think.

Talking Finance With Friends

Start by being direct. Before rent is due, send a simple message like, *"Hey, can we go over the rent split before the first so we all know the plan?"* It keeps the tone neutral and removes the guesswork. For utilities, try something short and friendly: *"Hi all. The electric bill is $82 this month, so $20.50 each. Please send by Friday so we avoid late fees. Thanks!"* Nobody feels called out because you are giving information, not accusations.

If someone misses a payment, keep the emotion out of it. A simple, *"Hey [roommate], I did not see your part come through yet. Do you need the payment link again?"* gives them space to fix it without feeling attacked. If the late payments become a pattern, shift into a problem-solving approach: *"I noticed the bills have been running late. Is there a reminder system that would work better for everyone?"* You are looking for solutions, not blame.

Loaning money to friends is trickier because you want your money back without looking like a debt collector. Try, *"Hey, just checking in about the $30 from last week. When will it work for you to send it?"* It is clear and respectful. If they keep dodging it, get more specific: *"Money has been tight for me, too. Can we set a date that works for payback so I can plan around it?"* Directness protects the friendship more than silence ever will.

Talking Finance With Family and Partners

Talking money with family can feel even heavier because history, expectations, and emotions get tangled up fast. When you need to ask your parents for support after graduation, be honest: *"I would like to talk about what support looks like after graduation. Can we sit down this week?"* You are not demanding anything. You are opening the door for a real conversation.

If you want to politely decline financial help, try, *"I really appreciate you offering. I want to try handling this myself for now. If I run into trouble, I will ask."* It shows gratitude while keeping your independence intact.

With partners, early conversations make a big difference. Whether you are splitting groceries or moving in together, get expectations on the table before frustration builds. *"Can we talk about how we want to split shared expenses so we both feel comfortable?"* is a great opener. If you regularly spend money together, discuss limits beforehand: *"Do we want to check in with each other on purchases over a certain amount?"* No drama. No surprises.

Here is something I learned the hard way: Money talks feel terrible when you keep everything in your head. Years ago, I assumed someone knew they owed me money because it seemed obvious. I waited. Then waited more. Turns out they did not know. When I finally brought it up calmly, it took them about ten seconds to pay me because they thought they had already sent it. That moment taught me that clear words solve problems faster than silent frustration.

Before any money conversation, use this quick checklist:

Quick-Prep Checklist: Before You Talk Money

- Know what you want: payment, clarity, or a new rule.
- Gather any numbers or receipts.
- Pick a good time to talk (not midnight or during finals).
- Practice your main points once or twice.
- Remember that you deserve clarity.
- Pause if things get heated and suggest continuing later.
- Have alternatives ready, such as a payment plan or calendar reminders.

If someone gets defensive, return to your experience instead of pointing fingers. Instead of *"You never pay on time,"* say, *"I get stressed when bills run late because I do not want us getting hit with fees."* It keeps the tone calm and honest.

Money conversations might feel awkward at first, but they build trust, respect, and better relationships. They prevent resentment, keep friendships intact, and save you from being the only one covering the Wi-Fi bill while everyone else streams guilt-free. The more you practice, the easier it gets, and before long, you become the surprisingly calm, organized person others turn to when group money decisions happen.

You do not need perfect words, just honest ones. Every conversation is a step toward stronger communication and fewer financial surprises. And trust me—that is a skill worth having long after the group chats fade and the shared apartments are behind you.

Negotiating Like a Pro: From Your First Job Offer to Monthly Bills

Negotiation is not just something CEOs do in glass offices. You already negotiate more than you think. Maybe you ask for extra sauce, try to swap shifts at work, or convince your friends to watch literally anything other than the same superhero reboot for the fifth time. Those tiny everyday negotiations use the same skills you need for the bigger stuff like your salary, rent, bills, or phone plan. Feeling nervous is normal, but you do not need to become a smooth talker or pretend you have your life perfectly together. Good negotiation is really about preparation, clarity, and speaking up without apologizing for existing.

I learned this the day I tried negotiating a used car price right after college. I walked in rehearsing lines like I was auditioning for a play, but all that buildup came down to simply asking, *"Can you do any better on that number?"* The salesperson thought for a second, shrugged, and dropped the price by a couple hundred dollars. No dramatic speech needed. I remember thinking, *Wait... that worked?* That tiny moment taught me that most negotiation is just asking calmly and seeing what happens.

Your first job offer is usually the moment you realize adults were not joking when they said money conversations can feel awkward. You get the call: *"We would like to offer you $61,000 a year."* Your heart screams yes. Your brain whispers, *"Wait, what if this is their low number?"* What most young adults don't know is that employers almost always expect you to negotiate. They won't be offended if you ask. They will probably be more surprised if you don't.

Before responding, do some research. Look up similar roles in your city on Glassdoor or Indeed, and check the typical benefits for your field. That way, when you respond with something like, *"Thank you for the offer. Based on my research and my experience with [skill], I was hoping for something closer to $65,000,"* you sound informed instead of demanding. You are starting a conversation, not re-enacting a courtroom drama.

If you prefer email because it gives you time to breathe and reword things seventeen times before sending, try:

Hi [Hiring Manager's Name],

Thank you so much for the offer. I am excited about the opportunity to join your team and I believe my background and experience would make me a strong fit for [Company Name]. Based on my research and my experience with [specific project or skill], I would like to know if there is flexibility to discuss a starting salary in the range of $65,000. I am also open to discussing other benefits or adjustments that would make the package work well for both of us.

Warm regards,
[Your Name]

Sometimes they really cannot budge on salary. That is when you channel your inner menu-substitution expert and start asking about other benefits. More vacation time, a signing bonus, flexible scheduling, training stipends, you name it. Employers appreciate someone who advocates for themselves kindly and confidently.

Negotiation does not disappear once you start the job. When you take on more responsibility, deliver results, or solve problems, it is fair to ask for your compensation to reflect it. Schedule a meeting and treat it like you are presenting a highlight reel. "In the past year, I led two projects, improved our workflow, trained new staff, and helped boost client satisfaction. I would like to discuss adjusting my compensation to reflect these contributions." No rambling. No apologizing. Just clarity and confidence. If they cannot do it now, ask when you can revisit or what milestones they want to see.

Freelancers know negotiation well because they live in a world where someone will inevitably message, "Can you do this entire project for $20?" A calm reply works wonders. "Given the scope and my experience, my rate is $X. If that is above your budget, I can offer a smaller deliverable." Translation: I respect your wallet, but I respect my time, too.

Negotiating Grown-Up Expenses

You will also negotiate in everyday life. When your internet bill decides to randomly increase for no reason, call customer service and say, "I noticed my bill went up. I am seeing similar plans from other companies for $10 less. Can you match that or offer a better rate?" You would be shocked at how often they say yes. Most companies would rather keep you as a customer than explain your cancellation to their boss.

Phone plans, insurance policies, subscription services, the price of streaming bundles that never stop multiplying—all of these can be negotiated. You just need a little data and a polite, direct question.

Rent is another area where negotiation can save you a lot. If your lease is coming up and similar apartments nearby are listed for less, show your landlord a couple of examples and say, "I have always paid on time and taken good care of the place. Would you consider keeping the rent the same or adjusting it slightly?" Most landlords prefer a reliable tenant over the risk of leaving the place empty. One of my old landlords practically threw confetti when I renewed because he did not want to deal with more viewings.

You will also negotiate in group settings, sometimes without realizing it. A friend of mine planned a spring break trip for a group where everyone had wildly different budgets. She made a quick spreadsheet listing estimated costs. Then everyone anonymously voted on what they cared about most. The group found a plan that fit every budget without drama or passive-aggressive sighs. That is negotiation too: getting clear information and making decisions that respect everyone involved.

Before any negotiation, use this simple prep checklist:

Negotiation Prep Checklist

- Research typical pay rates or prices.
- Know your ideal outcome and your minimum acceptable one.
- Practice asking aloud or typing it out.
- Frame requests collaboratively.
- Prepare alternatives if they cannot meet your request.
- Be willing to walk away if the terms truly are not fair.
- Get the agreement in writing.
- Read everything carefully before signing.

Negotiation will not always feel smooth. You might stumble, over-think your phrasing, or replay the conversation in your mind like a movie trailer. That is part of learning. The more you do it, the more natural it becomes. Over time, you will look back and wonder why you ever felt nervous speaking up for yourself.

Good negotiation affects more than your paycheck. It shapes how you ask for help, set boundaries, and show others you value your time and energy. You are allowed to ask for what is fair. You are allowed to say no. Every time you speak up, even slightly awkwardly, you get better.

Negotiation is not about being pushy or trying to "win." It is everyday self-advocacy, and it pays off in your first job offer, your next raise, and even the moment you call your internet company and ask why your bill suddenly looks like a car payment. Once you realize you can negotiate successfully, you'll start seeing opportunities everywhere.

Creating Your Personalized, Doable Financial Roadmap

Think about next year, five years from now, or even ten years out. What does financial freedom look like for you? Maybe you want to break the paycheck-to-paycheck cycle, move out on your own, or finally build a savings cushion so you can sleep without worrying that one surprise bill will ruin everything. Or maybe you are dreaming big. A debt-free life. Your own place. A bank account balance that does not make you nervous when you open your banking app. Long-term goals can feel far away when you are just trying to make it through the week, but mapping things out makes them real and surprisingly doable.

MONEY TIMELINE

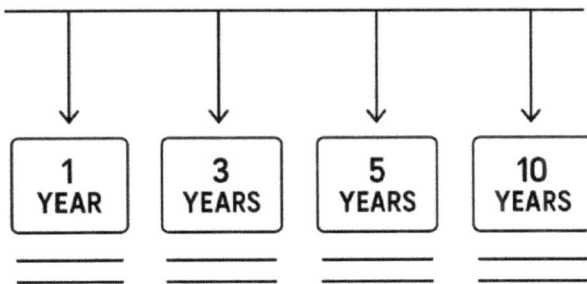

1 YEAR	3 YEARS	5 YEARS	10 YEARS

Start simple. Grab a notebook or open a new note on your phone and write, "Where do I want to be in one year?" Let yourself be honest without overthinking. Maybe you want a $1,000 emergency fund. Maybe you want your credit card balance gone. Maybe you want to make one small investment, even if it is only $25 or $50. Then look ahead five years. A smaller student loan balance. A better credit score. The savings to move to a new city. Then look ten years out and let yourself imagine a life with more options rather than limitations. If daydreaming is not your strength, picture the moment you check your balance and do not immediately whisper "please be okay" under your breath. Progress can feel like that.

Once your goals are written down, build a timeline. It does not have to be fancy. Draw a line and place your milestones along it. For example, "2026: $500 emergency fund. 2027: start Roth IRA. 2028: finish paying off credit card. 2029: trip to Japan." You want to give yourself visible targets. If you like visuals, use color-coded sticky notes or apps like Trello or Notion. Whatever helps you see the path is worth doing. I once stuck my own money goals on my fridge. Seeing them next to a half-empty bottle of ketchup somehow made them feel more official.

The Big, Scary Goals

Big goals can feel scary because they sound huge. Breaking them into small actions makes them manageable. If you want to save $1,000 in a year, that is around $20 a week. That might mean skipping one takeout meal, selling something you do not use, or picking up an extra shift once a month. Those tiny steps matter more than they seem. Every time you save even $5 or $10, you prove to yourself that progress is happening. Small wins build real momentum.

Keeping momentum is easier when you have a routine. Create a checklist for monthly, quarterly, and yearly check-ins. Each month, look at your spending categories and move any extra money toward savings. Every three months, check your progress on bigger goals like debt payoff or vacation savings. Once a year, do a full "money audit." List all your assets and debts, add up your net worth, and review what worked well. A friend of mine saved $500 by setting a $10 weekly transfer and giving herself a five-minute Sunday night check-in. She joked that it was like watering a plant. A small weekly effort keeps the whole thing alive.

Accountability also helps. Do not rely on memory alone. Set reminders in your phone. Make a monthly event called "Money Check-in" and treat it like an important appointment. Review accounts, scan for surprise charges, adjust your budget, and celebrate small victories. Or get a "money buddy." Text each other once a month and ask, "How are you doing on your goals?" Then share any wins or setbacks. Encouragement goes a long way. Plus, it is nice to have someone else who understands the thrill of saving an unexpected $10.

Simple Example of a Check-in Schedule

- **First Sunday:** Review all accounts.
- **Second Sunday:** Update budget based on actual spending.
- **Third Sunday:** Check progress on long-term goals.
- **Fourth Sunday:** Reflect on challenges and set next month's action steps.

Learning about money is also part of the roadmap. Self-advocacy means asking questions, even basic ones, whenever something confuses you. Use podcasts like The Ramsey Show, So Money, or Planet Money for simple explanations. Watch YouTube channels that teach financial basics without trying to hype you into something you do not need. Books and blogs also help. Build your skills month by month. Maybe one month you learn about credit utilization, and the next month you dive into Roth IRAs. Little by little, your financial vocabulary grows.

Celebrate your wins along the way. Do not wait until you finish everything on your list. When you hit a savings goal or pay off a credit card, treat yourself responsibly. A nice coffee. A movie night. A small outing with friends. At the end of the year, make a list of your money wins—big and small. You might be surprised by how much progress you have made. Even recognizing that you stuck to a routine more consistently counts as a win.

Life moves fast in your twenties and early thirties. Jobs change. Roommates move out. Relationships shift. Goals evolve. That is normal. Give yourself permission to adjust your plan without guilt. Maybe you need to pause investing for a few months or rebuild your emergency fund after a big expense. Being flexible is not failure. It is part of how real people succeed long term.

Consistency Beats Perfection Every Time

There is no single right path. What matters is having direction and sticking with small steps that fit your real life. Consistency beats perfection every time. If you feel stuck, return to your timeline and checklists. Remind yourself how far you have already come. Every dollar saved and every good decision is proof that you are moving forward.

This roadmap will help you gain control. When you know where you are going and how you will get there, money stops feeling like the villain in your story and starts becoming the helpful tool it should be.

As you wrap up this book, pause and acknowledge your progress. You are thinking about your future, planning for it, and taking real steps.

That alone puts you ahead of a lot of people who keep waiting for the "right time" to start.

You are building something solid, one step at a time, and those steps really do add up.

Conclusion

If you are reading this, take a second and give yourself some credit. I mean, really, pause for a moment. You picked up a book about money, pushed past the doubts or stress you felt in the beginning, and made it all the way to the end. Most people never even start. You did, and that matters. You began with questions, maybe even worries about whether you were doing this "adult money thing" right. Now you have real tools, real strategies, and a clearer understanding of how money fits into your life. That is progress. And it is a big deal.

Think back to where you were at the beginning. Maybe you felt confused about basic terms. Maybe you were worried about making mistakes. Maybe you wondered if you were the only one who did not "get" this stuff. And now you know something important: Confusion is normal, mistakes are common, and learning is always possible. You learned how to trade panic for planning and how to replace "I am bad with money" with "I am figuring this out." That shift alone can change your entire financial path.

We covered a lot together. You learned how digital banking works and how to set up accounts that support your goals instead of complicating your life. You practiced budgeting methods and figured out which ones fit your personality. You learned how small habits, like tracking subscriptions or automating savings, can change everything without forcing you to live like a monk.

You learned how credit works and how to build it without falling into common traps. You learned how to deal with student loans in a way that feels manageable instead of overwhelming. You built a starter plan for saving and investing so your future is not just something you hope for but something you actively create.

You learned how to protect yourself online, how to spot scams before they happen, and what steps to take if things go sideways. You learned how to have real conversations about money with roommates, friends, partners, and employers. Those skills alone will save you from stress, frustration, and arguments you do not need in your life.

You learned how to negotiate with more confidence. You learned how to map out your goals, break them down into small steps, and create a personal money roadmap you can adapt as life changes. And it will change. That is normal. And remember: The goal is steady progress that fits the real world you live in, *not* perfection.

Here is something I want you to tuck away and remember: You do not need to do everything all at once. You do not need to master money overnight. Financial literacy is not a finish line. It is a skill you build over time. Anyone can learn this, and you already have. Every responsible choice, every question you ask, and every new habit you practice is a step in the right direction.

So here is your final challenge. Choose one action from this book and do it within the next 48 hours. One small thing. Set up a budget. Pull your credit report. Automate $10 into savings. Talk to a roommate about bills. Pick something simple and doable. Small wins stack up fast, and momentum builds confidence.

Stay curious as you continue learning. Keep asking questions. Follow creators who teach money in a way you enjoy. Listen to a podcast during your commute. Try a budgeting app. Share what you learn with friends. Being open about money makes everyone stronger.

And when setbacks happen, because they will, take a breath and reset. Overspend one month? Try again. Miss a savings target? Adjust and move forward. Everyone slips sometimes. What matters is that you do not quit on yourself.

Most importantly, remember that your financial roadmap does not have to look like anyone else's. It belongs to you. You get to decide what stability looks like. You get to decide what freedom means. You get to build a future that feels secure and hopeful and genuinely yours.

I wrote this book because financial confidence is something anyone can build when they understand the basics. You've already taken the kind of steady, intentional steps that eventually turn into independence and long-term success.

You are putting yourself in a stronger position with every choice you make. You're learning how to protect yourself, how to plan realistically, and how to align your money with the future you want. That momentum matters.

Here's to the next chapter you create—one shaped by clarity, calm, and more control than you've ever had before.

You have everything it takes.

You've got this.

References

96% of Americans believe at least one money myth. (2021). *LendingTree.* https://www.lendingtree.com/personal/financial-literacy-survey/

An essential guide to building an emergency fund. (2024). *Consumer Financial Protection Bureau.* https://www.consumerfinance.gov/an-essential-guide-to-building-an-emergency-fund/

Annual Credit Report.com – Home page. (2025). *Annual Credit Report.* https://www.annualcreditreport.com/index.action

Bankrate. (2025). *9 best money saving apps of 2025.* https://www.bankrate.com/personal-finance/best-money-saving-apps/

Bankrate. (2025, July). *Best secured credit cards to build credit in July 2025.* https://www.bankrate.com/credit-cards/building-credit/best-secured-cards/

Baker Boyer Bank. (2025). *Building financial confidence and investing in yourself.* https://www.bakerboyer.com/resources/articles/building-financial-confidence-and-investing-in-yourself

Bruneida. (2025). *Envelope budgeting system | Everything else for sale in Brunei* [Listing no. 76603]. https://www.bruneida.com/Envelope-budgeting-system-76603

Business Insider. (2023, July). *"Bougie broke" is the latest financial trend sweeping...* https://www.businessinsider.com/bougie-broke-trend-luxury-living-during-cost-of-living-crisis-2023-7

Cape Cod 5. (2022). *Common scams targeting Gen Z – Red flags & how to avoid them.* https://www.capecodfive.com/resources/common-scams-targeting-gen-z-red-flags-how-avoid-them

CISA. (n.d.). *Cybersecurity best practices.* https://www.cisa.gov/topics/cybersecurity-best-practices

CNBC Select. (2024). *What are sinking funds and should you have them?* https://www.cnbc.com/select/what-are-sinking-funds/

College Raptor. (2025). *5 student loan apps for paying off debt faster.* https://www.collegeraptor.com/paying-for-college/articles/student-loans/apps-to-help-pay-off-student-loans/

Consumer Financial Protection Bureau. (2022). *Creating a savings first aid kit.* https://files.consumerfinance.gov/f/documents/cfpb_building_block_activities_creating-savings-first-aid-kit_guide.pdf

Consumer Financial Protection Bureau. (n.d.). *Financial planning worksheet: My new money goal.* https://files.consumerfinance.gov/f/documents/cfpb_my-new-money-goal_worksheet.pdf

Consumer Financial Protection Bureau. (2022). *Understanding paycheck deductions.* https://files.consumerfinance.gov/f/documents/cfpb_building_block_activities_understanding-paycheck-deductions_handout.pdf

Esade. (2022, November 2). *How fintech can foster financial inclusion and literacy.* *Forbes.* https://www.forbes.com/sites/esade/2022/11/02/how-fintech-can-foster-financial-inclusion-and-literacy/

Federal Deposit Insurance Corporation. (2021, December). *Overdraft and account fees.* https://www.fdic.gov/consumer-resource-center/2021-12/overdraft-and-account-fees

GoBankingRates. (2024). *8 best mobile banking apps of 2024.* https://www.gobankingrates.com/banking/technology/best-mobile-banking-apps-services/

Harvard Business Review. (2014, April). *15 rules for negotiating a job offer.* https://hbr.org/2014/04/15-rules-for-negotiating-a-job-offer

IdentityTheft.gov. (n.d.). *U.S. Federal Trade Commission.* https://www.identitytheft.gov/

Investopedia. (2024). *8 common investing mistakes to avoid.* https://www.investopedia.com/articles/stocks/07/beat_the_mistakes.asp

Investopedia. (2024). *How is my credit score calculated?* https://www.investopedia.com/ask/answers/05/creditscorecalculation.asp

Investopedia. (2025). *The best IRA for a 20-something investor.* https://www.investopedia.com/ask/answers/08/20s-best-kind-ira.asp

Investopedia. (2025). *Top 10 personal finance podcasts.* https://www.investopedia.com/top-10-personal-finance-podcasts-5088034

Kiplinger. (2024). *Eight tips for managing fluctuating income.* https://www.kiplinger.com/personal-finance/tips-for-managing-fluctuating-income

MassMutual. (2025). *What are payday loans and how do they work?* https://blog.massmutual.com/planning/dangers-payday-loans

My Horizon Credit Union. (2019). *Scripts for talking about money with those we love.* https://www.myhorizoncu.com/love-and-money-scripts-for-talking-about-money-with-those-we-love/

NASAA. (2025). *Compound interest.* https://www.nasaa.org/investor-education/young-adult-money-mission/compound-interest-2/

NerdWallet. (2025). *How to choose the right budget system.* https://www.nerdwallet.com/article/finance/how-to-choose-the-right-budget-system

NerdWallet. (2025). *10 Ways to Pay Off Credit Card Debt* https://www.nerdwallet.com/article/finance/credit-card-debt

NerdWallet. (2025). *The best budget apps for 2025: YNAB, PocketGuard and more.* https://www.nerdwallet.com/article/finance/best-budget-apps

NerdWallet. (2025). *What do you need to open a bank account?* https://www.nerdwallet.com/article/banking/how-to-open-a-bank-account-what-you-need

NerdWallet. (2025). *9 Best Investment Apps for Beginners.* https://www.nerdwallet.com/best/investing/investment-apps

PCMag. (2025). *Trim the fat: How to better track and manage paid subscriptions.* https://www.pcmag.com/how-to/track-and-manage-your-paid-subscriptions

Prograd. (n.d.). *Free money-making sites for students.* https://www.prograd.uk/blog/free-money-making-sites-for-students

162

Research.com. (2025). *Top 255 stores that offer student discounts for 2025.* https://research.com/education/top-stores-that-give-a-student-discounts

Studentaid.gov. (n.d.). *Federal versus private loans.* https://studentaid.gov/understand-aid/types/loans/federal-vs-private

Studentaid.gov. (n.d.). *Loan simulator.* https://studentaid.gov/loan-simulator

Studentaid.gov. (n.d.). *Manage loans.* https://studentaid.gov/h/manage-loans

Studentaid.gov. (n.d.). *Public Service Loan Forgiveness (PSLF).* https://studentaid.gov/manage-loans/forgiveness-cancellation/public-service

TwentyTwo13. (2024). *YOLO and FOMO: Ways to navigate modern-day temptations.* https://twentytwo13.my/yolo-and-fomo-ways-to-navigate-modern-day-temptations/

Vertex42. (2021). *Zero-based budget worksheet.* https://www.vertex42.com/ExcelTemplates/zero-based-budget-worksheet.html

Bonus Section

Budget Templates

Template 1: 50/30/20 Budget Planner

*Divide your monthly take-home pay into Needs (50%), Wants (30%), and Savings/Debt (20%)

Category	Description	Planned	Actual	Difference
	Income	**$0**	**$0**	
Needs (50%)	Rent	$0	$0	$0
	Utilities	$0	$0	$0
	Groceries	$0	$0	$0
	Transportation	$0	$0	$0
	Phone	$0	$0	$0
		$0	$0	$0
Wants (30%)	Dining Out	$0	$0	$0
	Streaming	$0	$0	$0
	Clothing	$0	$0	$0
	Hobbies	$0	$0	$0
	Gym	$0	$0	$0
	Fun	$0	$0	$0
		$0	$0	$0
Savings (20%)	Debt Payments (Student Loan)	$0	$0	$0
	Savings Account	$0	$0	$0
	Savings TBD	$0	$0	$0
		$0	$0	$0
	Total Expenses	**$0**	**$0**	**$0**

Template 2: Pay-Yourself-First Budget Planner

*Move money automatically toward your goals before paying any bills.

*Whatever remains covers needs and wants.

Category	Description	Planned	Actual
	Income	**$0**	**$0**
SAVINGS	Savings TBD	$0	$0
	Roth IRA	$0	$0
	Debt Repayment	$0	$0
	Other	$0	$0
	Total Savings	$0	$0
	Remaining After Saving	**$0**	**$0**
NEEDS	Rent	$0	$0
	Utilities	$0	$0
	Groceries	$0	$0
	Phone	$0	$0
	Transportation	$0	$0
	Other	$0	$0
	Total Needs	$0	$0
	Remaining After Needs	**$0**	**$0**
WANTS	Dining Out	$0	$0
	Streaming	$0	$0
	Subscriptions	$0	$0
	Coffee	$0	$0
	Fun	$0	$0
	Other	$0	$0
	Total Wants	$0	$0
	Remaining After Wants	**$0**	**$0**

Template 3: Zero-Based Budget Planner

List all income and expenses until Income - Expense =$0.

Every dollar gets a job.

Income	$0	$0	
Description	**Planned**	**Actual**	**Difference**
Rent	$0	$0	$0
Utilities	$0	$0	$0
Groceries	$0	$0	$0
Phone	$0	$0	$0
Transportation	$0	$0	$0
Streaming	$0	$0	$0
Dining Out	$0	$0	$0
Fun	$0	$0	$0
Clothing	$0	$0	$0
Savings 1	$0	$0	$0
Savings 2	$0	$0	$0
Credit Card 1	$0	$0	$0
Credit Card 2	$0	$0	$0
Debt Payment	$0	$0	$0
Other	$0	$0	$0
Total Expenses	**$0**	**$0**	**$0**
Income - Expenses	**$0**	**$0**	**$0**

Scenario Solutions

Scenario 1: Josh & the Family Vacation (50/30/20 Budget)

		1	2	3
	Income	**$2,400**	**$2,400**	**$2,400**
Category	**Description**	**Planned**	**Planned**	**Planned**
Needs (50%)	Rent	$800	$800	$800
	Utilities	$50	$50	$50
	Groceries	$200	$200	$200
	Transportation	$50	$50	$50
	Phone	$100	$100	$100
		$1,200	$1,200	$1,200
Wants (30%)	Dining Out	$250	$200	$200
	Streaming	$80	$80	$80
	Clothing	$150	$100	$100
	Hobbies	$100	$100	$100
	Gym	$60	$60	$60
	Fun	$80	$60	$60
		$720	$600	$600
Savings (20%)	Debt Payments (Student Loan)	$280	$280	$280
	Savings Account	$100	$20	$20
	Savings TBD	$100	$0	$0
	Family Vacation	$0	$300	$300
		$480	$600	$600
	Total Expenses	**$2,400**	**$2,400**	**$2,400**

*Fixed essentials stay consistent
*Trimmed $120/month in wants (months 2/3) to free up travel savings
*Shifted $180/month from Savings Account/Savings TBD to Family Vacation
*Budget balanced each month

Josh's plan works because he did not overhaul his entire life. He simply adjusted his priorities. By trimming about $120 a month from his wants and moving that money into savings, he built a travel fund that covered his $600 vacation in two months. His essentials stayed covered, he still kept space for fun, and he continued making steady progress on savings and debt. It is a great example of how the 50/30/20 method can flex when life changes. The real takeaway is this: budgeting is not about restriction. It is about choice and control. Josh proved you do not need a miracle or a second job to reach your goals. Sometimes a few small tweaks get you where you want to go.

Scenario 2: Samantha's Pay Raise (Pay-Yourself-First)

		1	2	3
	Income	**$1,800**	**$2,400**	**$2,400**
Category	**Description**	**Planned**	**Planned**	**Planned**
SAVINGS	Car Fund	$200	$500	$500
	Retirement	$100	$200	$200
	Debt Repayment	$100	$200	$200
	Other	$0	$0	$0
	Total Savings	$400	$900	$900
	Remaining After Saving	**$1,400**	**$1,500**	**$1,500**
NEEDS	Rent	$750	$750	$750
	Utilities	$50	$50	$50
	Groceries	$250	$250	$250
	Phone	$40	$40	$40
	Transportation	$25	$25	$25
	Other	$0	$0	$0
	Total Needs	$1,115	$1,115	$1,115
	Remaining After Needs	**$285**	**$385**	**$385**
WANTS	Dining Out	$150	$150	$150
	Streaming	$50	$50	$50
	Subscriptions	$25	$35	$35
	Coffee	$25	$50	$50
	Fun	$35	$100	$100
	Other	$0	$0	$0
	Total Wants	$285	$385	$385
	Remaining After Wants	**$0**	**$0**	**$0**

*Samantha's goal of owning her own car is getting closer.
*She increased her retirement contribution helping her account grow faster.
*She is paying her debts off sooner.
*She added to her wants to treat herself.

170

Samantha's plan works because she made her raise work for her instead of letting it quietly disappear into extra spending. As soon as her income went up, she boosted her savings, retirement contributions, and debt payments. By doing this right away, she avoided the classic "I earned more, so I'll spend more" trap that catches a lot of people off guard. The Pay-Yourself-First method helped her flip the script. Instead of saving whatever might be left at the end of the month, she saved first and lived on the rest. That simple change moved her closer to buying her own car, sped up her debt payoff, grew her retirement faster, and still gave her room to treat herself. It is a smart, sustainable way to build long-term stability without sacrificing every fun thing in the process.

Scenario 3: Alex's Job Loss (Zero-Based Budget)

	1	2	3
Income	**$1,600**	**$1,800**	**$800**
Description	**Planned**	**Planned**	**Planned**
Rent	$600	$600	$600
Utilities	$50	$50	$50
Groceries	$200	$200	$100
Phone	$90	$90	$50
Transportation	$60	$60	$0
Streaming	$75	$75	$0
Dining Out	$200	$250	$0
Fun	$50	$100	$0
Clothing	$0	$0	$0
Savings 1	$50	$100	$0
Savings 2	$0	$0	$0
Credit Card 1	$50	$100	$0
Credit Card 2	$50	$50	$0
Debt Payment	$125	$125	$0
Other	$0	$0	$0
Total Expenses	**$1,600**	**$1,800**	**$800**
Income - Expenses	**$0**	**$0**	**$0**

*The extra income in month 2 allows Alex to indulge slightly.
*He increased his dining out and fun budgets while also upping his savings and credit card payments.
*In month 3, Alex is now stripping his expenses to the bare bones.
*He starts calling his creditors and requesting deferral payments.
*Since his part-time job is gone, he doesn't need to budget for transportation.
*His cousin will cover the streaming cost for now since they both use Alex's TV.
*His prior savings can cover any small gaps.
*He starts to network his students looking for more needy pupils.

Alex's situation shows how quickly life can shift and how important it is to stay grounded when things change. When his income dropped, he did not freeze or ignore the problem. He shifted into a zero-based mindset and focused on what mattered most. By trimming his budget to the essentials, calling creditors early, and accepting temporary help from his cousin, he kept control during a stressful moment instead of letting the situation control him.

What made the biggest difference was his willingness to act quickly. He adjusted his spending, cut non-essentials, and relied on the savings he had set aside during better months. Zero-Based Budgeting gave him a clear structure to follow when his income changed, and every dollar had a purpose. Even when the numbers were tight, Alex stayed proactive and flexible.

His story is a good reminder that financial setbacks do not have to knock you off course. With honesty, communication, and a realistic plan, you can weather the low-income months and rebuild once things improve. Alex stayed afloat because he stayed engaged, and that is the real win here.

Bonus - Downloadable Budget Spreadsheets

Use this link for budget spreadsheets if you have a Google account and want to save the file to your Google Drive:

https://docs.google.com/spreadsheets/d/1qm1dFzLzTC-gGIOd j3YzQobc6ggkYMBR/copy

Use this link for budget spreadsheets if you have Microsoft Excel:

https://docs.google.com/spreadsheets/d/1qm1dFzLzTC-gGIOd j3YzQobc6ggkYMBR/export?format=xlsx

Extras

MONTHLY SPENDING AUDIT WORKSHEET

Goal: Spot where your money actually goes, so you can make smarter tweaks next month.
Instructions: Review your transactions from the past 30 days, sort them into categories, and total each one honestly.

Category	Total Spent	Surprised (Y/N)	Keep/Reduce/Cut
Food & Dining			
Groceries			
Transportation/Gas			
Subscriptions			
Streaming			
Shopping/Clothing			
Entertainment/Fun			
Health & Fitness			
Utilities & Bills			
Coffee/Snacks/Fast Food			
Total Monthly Spending	**$0.00**		

Reflect:
Which categories surprised you the most?
What was one expense that felt "worth it"?
What was one you regret or barely remember?
What's one small change you can make next month?

Pro Tip: Do this once a month. You'll start noticing patterns like that "one-time" food delivery that happens four times a week.

Apps and Tools

Category	App Name	What It Does	Platform(s)	Cost / Notes
		Apps & Tools for Everyday Financial Success		
Automated Savings	Digit	Analyzes spending and saves small daily amounts automatically	iOS, Android	Subscription
Automated Savings	Qapital	Automates saving using custom rules (roundups, habits)	iOS, Android	$3–$12/month
Budgeting	EveryDollar	Simple budget tracker	iOS, Android	Free + Paid
Budgeting	Goodbudget	Envelope-style system	iOS, Android, Web	Free + Paid
Budgeting	PocketGuard	Tracks spending and shows how much is safe to spend	iOS, Android	Free + Paid
Budgeting	Rocket Money	Tracks bills, finds subscriptions	iOS, Android	Free + Paid
Budgeting	Splitwise	Splits and tracks shared expenses with friends/roommates	iOS, Android, Web	Free + Paid
Budgeting	YNAB	Zero-based budgeting app	iOS, Android, Web	Subscription
Credit & Debt	Chase Credit Journey	Free credit monitoring and score tracking through Experian	iOS, Android, Web	Free
Credit & Debt	Credit Karma	Monitors credit scores	iOS, Android	Free
Credit & Debt	Experian Boost	Adds bills to credit report	iOS, Android	Free
Credit & Debt	Undebt.it	Tracks debt payoff	Web	Free
Digital Banking	Ally Bank	Online bank with great savings tools	iOS, Android, Web	Free
Digital Banking	Capital One	User-friendly with savings "buckets"	iOS, Android	Free
Digital Banking	Chime	Fee-free checking with early direct deposit	iOS, Android	Free
Digital Banking	SoFi	Combines banking, investing, and loans	iOS, Android	Free
Discounts (Student)	Student Beans	Student discounts and verification	iOS, Android, Web	Free
Discounts (Student)	UNiDAYS	Student-only discounts and deals	iOS, Android, Web	Free
Income & Side Hustles	Depop	Peer-to-peer resale marketplace	iOS, Android	Free
Income & Side Hustles	OfferUp	Local buy/sell marketplace; optional shipping; in-app messaging	iOS, Android, Web	Free (shipping fees)
Income & Side Hustles	Poshmark	Resale marketplace for clothing & goods	iOS, Android	Free
Investing & Saving	Acorns	Rounds up purchases to invest	iOS, Android	$3–$5/month
Investing & Saving	Betterment	Automated robo-advisor	iOS, Android	Fee-based
Investing & Saving	Public	Social investing platform	iOS, Android	Free
Investing & Saving	Robinhood	Commission-free stock investing	iOS, Android	Free
Job Search & Careers	Glassdoor	Company reviews, salaries, and job listings	iOS, Android, Web	Free
Job Search & Careers	Indeed	Job search engine and résumé posting	iOS, Android, Web	Free
Learning	Graham Stephan	YouTube channel explaining investing and personal finance	YouTube	Free
Learning	Planet Money	Entertaining economics podcast	All	Free
Learning	So Money	Financial interviews and tips	All	Free
Learning	The Financial Diet	Personal finance YouTube & blog for young adults	YouTube, Web	Free
Learning	The Ramsey Show	Real-world money podcast	All	Free
Payments	Cash App	Send money, buy Bitcoin	iOS, Android	Free
Payments	Venmo	Send and receive money	iOS, Android	Free
Payments	Zelle	Bank-integrated transfers	iOS, Android	Free
Productivity	Google Sheets	Create custom trackers	iOS, Android, Web	Free
Productivity	Notion	Custom planner/workspace	iOS, Android, Web	Free + Paid
Productivity	Trello	Visual task organizer	iOS, Android, Web	Free
Security & Password Mgmt	1Password	Secure password vault with family sharing and emergency access	iOS, Android, Web	Subscription
Security & Password Mgmt	Bitwarden	Open-source password manager with encrypted storage	iOS, Android, Web	Free + Paid
Security & Password Mgmt	Dashlane	Securely stores logins, generates strong passwords	iOS, Android, Web	Free + Paid
Self-Employment & Taxes	QuickBooks Self-Employed	Tracks income/expenses, mileage, quarterly taxes for freelancers	iOS, Android, Web	Subscription

Quiz

1. Why is the "pay yourself first" method so effective?

   a. It guarantees a raise from your employer
   b. It moves money into savings before you can spend it
   c. It eliminates the need for a budget
   d. It lowers your tax rate automatically

Answer: B

Paying yourself first automates saving so it happens consistently before impulse spending.

---

2. What is the primary purpose of an emergency fund?

   a. To cover unexpected expenses like car repairs or medical bills
   b. To buy things on sale
   c. To pay regular monthly subscriptions
   d. To invest in high-risk stocks

Answer: A

An emergency fund protects you from surprise costs so you don't need debt or panic when life happens.

---

3. Your paycheck shows a much higher gross pay than what lands in your bank. What best explains the difference?

    a. Your employer is secretly underpaying you
    b. Your bank is stealing your money
    c. Taxes and other deductions were taken out before deposit
    d. Your account has a hidden limit

Answer: C

The difference between gross and net pay comes from taxes and payroll deductions such as benefits or retirement.

---

4. You get a text saying "Your account is locked – click here to log in." What is the safest next step?

    a. Click the link and log in immediately
    b. Reply with your username to check
    c. Delete the text and ignore your account
    d. Call your bank using a verified phone number or app

Answer: D

Verifying through an official bank number prevents falling into a phishing scam.

---

5. What does zero-based budgeting actually mean?

    a. Every dollar of income is assigned a specific job
    b. You only track large expenses like rent and car payments
    c. You save only what is left at the end of the month
    d. You stop spending when your card is declined

Answer: A

Zero-based budgeting allocates every dollar to a purpose so none goes unaccounted for.

---

6. Which approach works best if your income changes from week to week?

    a. Spend freely and check your balance occasionally
    b. Build a budget based on your lowest reliable monthly income
    c. Ignore budgeting until your income is stable
    d. Put everything on a credit card and sort it out later

Answer: B

Budgeting using your minimum income keeps essentials covered even during slower periods.

---

7. Why can "buy now, pay later" plans be risky if you're not careful?

    a. They are illegal in most states
    b. They never show up on any statements
    c. They always charge 30% interest
    d. They break large purchases into small payments that can quietly pile up

Answer: D

Small installments disguise the real cost and encourage overspending across multiple purchases.

---

8. You're struggling to afford your student loan payments. What is the most productive first step?

  a. Stop paying and hope they forget
  b. Put the payments on a credit card
  c. Contact your loan servicer about lower or adjusted payments
  d. Take out another loan to cover them

Answer: C

Servicers can offer income-driven repayment, deferment, or forbearance to reduce short-term pressure.

---

9. Which habit is most helpful for building a strong credit history?

  a. Making payments on time every month
  b. Frequently maxing out your card
  c. Opening as many cards as possible
  d. Never checking your statements

Answer: A

Payment history is the biggest factor in your credit score and shows reliability to lenders.

---

10. Why is two-factor authentication (2FA) such an important security feature?

  a. It guarantees nobody can ever hack you
  b. It adds a second verification step beyond your password
  c. It replaces the need for passwords entirely
  d. It lets your bank watch all your activity

Answer: B

Two-factor authentication requires both a password and a separate code or device, making access harder for attackers.

---

11. Why does starting to invest in your teens or early 20s make such a big difference?

    a. Young investors avoid all taxes
    b. You can only invest when you're young
    c. More time allows compound interest to grow your money
    d. The stock market pays higher returns to younger people

Answer: C

Investing early gives your money more years to compound and multiply.

---

12. Which of the following is usually a good beginner-friendly investment option?

    a. Broad index funds or ETFs
    b. Random meme coins
    c. Single highly speculative stocks
    d. Lottery tickets

Answer: A

Index funds and ETFs diversify risk by spreading investments across many companies.

---

13. How can social media increase the temptation to overspend?

    a. It forces you to learn about stocks
    b. It blocks all financial content
    c. It gives detailed budgeting tips
    d. It shows highlight reels that make you feel like you're behind

Answer: D

Curated posts exaggerate others' lifestyles, encouraging comparison-driven spending.

---

14. Your credit score suddenly drops by a big amount and you don't know why. What should you do first?

    a. Open a new credit card to "fix" it
    b. Review your credit report for errors or suspicious accounts
    c. Close every account you have
    d. Ignore it and hope it goes back up

Answer: B

Examining the report reveals potential mistakes or fraud that may be pulling your score down.

---

15. Which type of student loan usually does not build up interest while you're in school?

    a. Private student loan
    b. Federal unsubsidized loan
    c. Federal subsidized loan
    d. Parent PLUS loan

Answer: C

The government pays interest on subsidized federal loans while you are enrolled at least half-time.

---

16. A roommate keeps forgetting to pay you back for their share of the utilities. What is the healthiest response?

    a. Keep paying it yourself and stay silent
    b. Call them out sarcastically in a group chat
    c. Move out without saying anything
    d. Have a calm conversation and set clear expectations and
       due dates

Answer: D

Direct, respectful communication prevents resentment and clarifies responsibilities.

---

17. Why is it dangerous to assume your friends' lifestyles online match their real finances?

    a. Everyone on social media is wealthy
    b. Only people with no debt post online
    c. Your feed shows everyone's full budget
    d. Posts highlight exciting moments, not credit card
       statements

Answer: D

Social media rarely shows financial stress or debt, just the best moments.

---

18. You receive a job offer that seems low for your role and area. How can you advocate for yourself effectively?

a. Accept it and complain later
b. Demand a much higher number with no explanation
c. Refuse to negotiate at all
d. Share salary research and ask if the offer can align more with market rates

Answer: D

Using market data allows you to negotiate professionally and increases your chance of a better offer.

---

19. What is a major risk of living paycheck-to-paycheck with no savings?

a. You'll automatically qualify for loans
b. You'll pay fewer taxes
c. One surprise expense can push you into debt
d. You'll never have to budget

Answer: C

Without a buffer, even small emergencies can lead to high-interest borrowing or missed bills.

---

20. Which feature should you absolutely expect from a solid banking app?

a. A built-in social feed
b. Strong security tools like alerts and biometric login

c. A bright color theme

d. The ability to buy lottery tickets

Answer: B

Banking tools must prioritize security to protect your accounts and identity.

www.ingramcontent.com/pod-product-compliance
Lightning Source LLC
Chambersburg PA
CBHW040924210326
41597CB00030B/5166